GREAT
FUNDRAISING
IDEAS
FOR YOUTH GROUPS

ZONDERVAN/YOUTH SPECIALTIES BOOKS

PROFESSIONAL RESOURCES

Advanced Peer Counseling in Youth Groups
Called to Care
Developing Student Leaders
Feeding Your Forgotten Soul
Great Fundraising Ideas for Youth Groups
Growing Up in America
Help! I'm a Volunteer Youth Worker!
High School Ministry
How to Recruit and Train Volunteer Youth Workers
　　(Previously released as Unsung Heroes)
Junior High Ministry (Revised Edition)
The Ministry of Nurture
Organizing Your Youth Ministry
Peer Counseling in Youth Groups
Road Trip
The Youth Minister's Survival Guide
Youth Ministry Nuts and Bolts

DISCUSSION STARTER RESOURCES

Amazing Tension Getters
Get 'Em Talking
High School TalkSheets
Hot Talks
Junior High TalkSheets
More High School TalkSheets
More Junior High TalkSheets
Option Plays
Parent Ministry TalkSheets
Teach 'Toons
Tension Getters
Tension Getters Two

SPECIAL NEEDS AND ISSUES

The Complete Student Missions Handbook
Divorce Recovery for Teenagers
Ideas for Social Action
Intensive Care: Helping Teenagers in Crisis
Rock Talk
Teaching the Truth About Sex
Up Close and Personal: How to Build Community
　　in Your Youth Group

YOUTH MINISTRY PROGRAMMING

Adventure Games
Creative Programming Ideas for Junior High Ministry
Creative Socials and Special Events
Good Clean Fun
Good Clean Fun, Volume 2

Great Games for City Kids
Great Ideas for Small Youth Groups
Greatest Skits on Earth
Greatest Skits on Earth, Volume 2
Holiday Ideas for Youth Groups (Revised Edition)
Junior High Game Nights
More Junior High Game Nights
On-Site: 40 On-Location Youth Programs
Play It! Great Games for Groups
Play It Again! More Great Games for Groups
Super Sketches for Youth Ministry
Teaching the Bible Creatively
The Youth Specialties Handbook for Great Camps and
　　Retreats

4TH-6TH GRADE MINISTRY

Attention Grabbers for 4th-6th Graders
4th-6th Grade TalkSheets
Great Games for 4th-6th Graders
How to Survive Middle School
Incredible Stories
More Attention Grabbers for 4th-6th Graders
More Great Games for 4th-6th Graders
More Quick and Easy Activities for 4th-6th Graders
Quick and Easy Activities for 4th-6th Graders
Teach 'Toons

CLIP ART

ArtSource™ Volume 1—Fantastic Activities
ArtSource™ Volume 2—Borders, Symbols, Holidays, and
　　Attention Getters
ArtSource™ Volume 3—Sports
ArtSource™ Volume 4—Phrases and Verses
ArtSource™ Volume 5—Amazing Oddities and Appalling
　　Images
ArtSource™ Volume 6—Spiritual Topics
Youth Specialties Clip Art Book
Youth Specialties Clip Art Book, Volume 2

VIDEO

Next Time I Fall in Love Video Curriculum
Understanding Your Teenager Video Curriculum
Video Spots for Junior High Game Nights

STUDENT BOOKS

Going the Distance
Grow for It Journal
Next Time I Fall in Love
Next Time I Fall in Love Journal

GREAT FUNDRAISING IDEAS

FOR YOUTH GROUPS

OVER 150 EASY-TO-USE
MONEY-MAKERS THAT REALLY WORK

DAVID & KATHY LYNN

Youth
Specialties

ZondervanPublishingHouse
Grand Rapids, Michigan

A Division of HarperCollins*Publishers*

Great Fundraising Ideas for Youth Groups
Copyright © 1993 by Youth Specialties, Inc.

Youth Specialties Books, 1224 Greenfield Drive, El Cajon, California 92021, are published by Zondervan Publishing House, Grand Rapids, Michigan 49530.

Library of Congress Cataloging-in-Publication Data

Lyn, David, 1954–
    Great fundraising ideas for youth groups : over 150 money-making ideas / David and Kathy Lynn.
       p.   cm.
    "Youth Specialties."
    Includes index.
    ISBN 0-310-67171-X (pbk.)
    1. Church work with teenagers.   2. Church fundraising.   I. Lynn, Kathy.   II. Title.
BV4447.L96   1993
254.8—dc20   93-7448
                                                 CIP

Interior design by JamisonBell Advertising & Design
Cover designed by Karen Johnson
Edited by Noel Becchetti and Jan Ortiz

Printed in the United States of America

93 94 95 96 97 /CH/ 10 9 8 7 6 5 4 3 2 1

DEDICATION

T**O ALL THOSE YOUTH WORKERS,** parents, grandparents, and friends and supporters of young people and youth work who have unselfishly given of their
time, energy and money to raise money so that youth work can continue
both within and outside the church. And a special thanks to all those with
whom we have worked to raise money to support the youth work in which
we have been involved.

DISCLAIMER

THIS BOOK (LIKE LIFE) CONTAINS ACTIVITIES that, in an unfortunate combination of circumstances, could result in emotional or physical harm. You'll need to evaluate each activity on its own merit for your group, for each one's potential risk, for safety precautions that must be taken, advance preparation that must be required, and possible results before you use any activity. Youth Specialties, Inc., Zondervan Publishing House, or David and Kathy Lynn are not responsible—nor have they any control over—the use or misuse of any of the activities published in this book.

CONTENTS

ACKNOWLEDGMENTS

SOME OF THE FUNDRAISING IDEAS FOUND IN THIS BOOK originally appeared in the Ideas Library, published by Youth Specialties, Inc. Others were collected by the authors from youth workers from around the country. And some originally appeared in articles in *New Designs for Youth Development* written by David and Kathy Lynn.

The authors wish to thank all of the following creative youth workers who originally developed these ideas and contributed them for publication. Without them, this book would not have been possible. Thanks again to: Bob Baker, Martin Barker, Linda Behrendt, Rick Bell, Frank Billman, Nancy Blanchard, Bradley Bergfalk, Kirk Bookout, Beth Brittain, Ridge Burns, Jim Burton, Kent Busman, Kaye Carew, Howard Chapman, Kerry Clenn, Gary Close, John Collins, Robert Crosby, Randy Deering, Scott Dell, Diane E. Deming, Dwight Douglas, Dallas Elder, Jim Elliott, Nancy Freyer, Cherie Friend, Dave Gilliam, Dave Griewe, Michael Gulotta, Danny Hansen, Dwight Heirendt, Bob Henry, Dave Hicks, Ruth Holste, Ray Houser, Larry Houseman, William C. Humphries, Jim Johnson, Len Kageler, Doug King, Geoffrey Koglin, Larry Lawrence, Keith Lowry, Steve Mabry, Bob Machovec, Terry O. Martinson, Mary Jo Mastin, Mary McKemy, Richard McPherson, Malcolm McQueen, Jerry Meadows, Arthur Merkle, Linda Miller, R. Albert Mohler, Jr., R. Michael Naron, Randy Nichols, E.J. Nusbaum, Don Orange, Ray Peterson, Randy Pierce, Lynn H. Pryor, Rodney Puryear, Mark Reierson, Rosalind Rhodes, Bill Robertson, Elaine Rowe, Jim Scott, Sean Smith, Don Snider, Larry D. Spicer, Dick Stiansen, Mike Stipe, John Stumbo, Jerry Summers, Ann C. Swallow, Doug Tensen, Warren Ueckert, Daniel Unrath, Roger Voskuil, Marv Walker, Wes Wesner, Ron Wells, Rick Wheeler, Donna Youmus, Mike Youmus.

INTRODUCTION

THIS BOOK WAS WRITTEN with the church and para-church youth worker in mind, although the fundraising ideas found here can also work with other youth-serving groups—school groups, scout troops, clubs, sports teams, after-school programs, and camps. Youth work encompasses many different types of groups. Thus, some fundraising ideas will appeal to one type of group who have a certain philosophy, while another type of fundraiser will appeal to a different group with a different philosophy.

The success of your fundraising event depends to a large extent on the effort you place in prayerfully choosing, planning and promoting your event. Many fundraisers fail because groups do not carefully analyze their past and current situations, missions, and goals. A haphazard approach to raising money will inevitably fail. It is not the idea that generates the funds, but the right idea at the right time coupled with the right cause.

Rushing to grab an idea or two that look like quick cash-getters can actually hurt your fundraising efforts. Your group will be raising funds without a plan or direction. You will benefit if you read the first two chapters before hunting for the fundraising ideas that look like good prospects for your group.

Treat yourself to an "ideas smorgasbord" by skimming through the ideas section of the book. As you survey the ideas, brainstorm how you might modify some of them to fit your particular group's needs. Think also of ways you can strengthen your already existing fundraising projects. Be as creative as you wish at modifying and strengthening the ideas you find in this book.

Happy fundraising!

SECTION ONE

A PRIMER FOR SUCCESSFUL AND ETHICAL FUNDRAISING

CHAPTER ONE

PLANNING A SUCCESSFUL FUNDRAISER

SUCCESSFUL FUNDRAISERS DON'T JUST HAPPEN. A great fundraiser includes a great plan. Use the following simple ingredients to help you carefully plan your next fundraiser.

STATE YOUR OPPORTUNITY

People give more freely to worthy causes or programs than they do to organizations. In order to assist people with their contributions, put together a clear, compelling statement that presents the opportunity you are offering. People need to be convinced that your cause is worthy of their support. The most successful fundraising efforts are those where the group has developed a written purpose statement (professional fundraisers often call this a case statement). Develop yours in such a way that it will enable all of your group members to articulate to prospective givers the reason for raising funds.

A good purpose statement tells people who you are (organizationally), why you are doing what you are doing, why you need their financial support, and how much money you will need. Your group members can now quickly and convincingly offer people the chance to participate in your ministry.

CHOOSE THE RIGHT FUNDRAISER

Out of the hundreds of ideas available to your group, which do you choose? There are no hard and fast rules, but here are some questions to help guide your thinking.

- How much money is it possible to raise?
- How much work will it take to raise the needed money?
- Is this idea in line with the philosophy and policies of our organization?
- Are there more effective ways to get the money we need?
- Do we have the resources available to adequately pull off this fundraiser?
- Is this the best time for our group to undertake this effort?
- How excited are we about this idea?
- What other groups have already used this fundraising idea?
- What fundraisers have been successful in the past? Are those ideas worth repeating at this time?

USE A TEAM APPROACH

People speak of fundraising as being a team sport, yet so often it works out to be an individual effort. If you are going to play, you need to play as a team. You don't need additional unreasonable expectations placed on your already overburdened shoulders. A well-defined fundraising plan that clearly and specifically spells out a team approach will help you avoid doing all the work yourself.

Everyone knows something about fundraising. And everyone brings their perspectives, ideas, even fears to the fundraising process. This is because fundraising has affected everyone in one way or another. Everyone has been a part of fundraising, as a donor (one who gives), a solicitor (one who persuades others to give), a receiver (one who benefits from the funds), or some combination of the three. People's past experiences with fundraising, be they good or bad, will help you as you assemble your fundraising team.

Six W's and an H will easily and effectively help any fundraising team create a workable plan that distributes the work throughout the team: *WHO* will do *WHAT* with *WHOM, WHY, WHERE, WHEN,* and *HOW?*

TEAM CHART

Use the chart on page 18 to help organize your team. First brainstorm. Decide which tasks will be necessary to make the fundraiser a success. Then solicit volunteers to carry out each of these tasks, setting the date when each task is to be completed. Finally, estimate the cost of completing each task. Fundraising costs can be kept to a minimum by utilizing talents of people in your group. For example, those with an artistic flair can contribute their expertise to create publicity products such as posters or flyers.

Name of Fundraiser _____

	Fundraising Task	Person(s) Responsible	Date to be Completed	Estimated Cost
1.	_____	_____	_____	_____
2.	_____	_____	_____	_____
3.	_____	_____	_____	_____
4.	_____	_____	_____	_____
5.	_____	_____	_____	_____
6.	_____	_____	_____	_____
7.	_____	_____	_____	_____
8.	_____	_____	_____	_____

SELECT A CHAIRPERSON

Find someone who will serve as a chairperson. A chairperson's responsibilities do not negate team effort; you'll find that a leader can coordinate your fundraiser and keep the team running smoothly. An often untapped resource in this regard are retired persons in your church or community. Many have extensive fundraising experience, having served on boards, or been involved in fundraising for various other agencies, churches and organizations.

PROMOTE YOUR FUNDRAISER

What looks on paper to be the most successful fundraiser ever, will be a disaster if promotion falls through. Failure to effectively promote a project will render it a waste of time and effort. Therefore, remind people again and again about your fundraiser. The best way to do this is by employing a variety of creative strategies. For example, a one-time plug for your after-church salad bar (see After-Church Salad Bar on page 55) virtually guarantees that few people will show up. However, if you combine this verbal plug with posters, a newsletter reminder, a phone chain, a bulletin insert, and a verbal reminder in all the Sunday school classes, the event is more likely to be a grand success.

A few art supplies, willing hands and a little creativity allow the cost of fundraising to be kept to a minimum. There is no need to spend large amounts of money to promote what you are doing. You will find a grab bag of inexpensive promotion ideas in Chapter Thirteen.

TIPS FOR SUCCESS

The following tidbits are essential to the success of your fundraising efforts:

SCOUT YOUR LOCATION. The right choice in facilities is important as is checking on the cost and availability. If you are holding an outdoor event, you will more than likely want to plan an alternative location in case of foul weather.

MAKE SURE YOU'RE IN LINE WITH RULES AND REGULATIONS. Many organizations have rules about fundraisers. For example, if your group is selling candy bars, other groups may appreciate knowing that, so that they are better able to plan their fundraisers. Two organizations selling the same thing in the same area will not have very much success.

STAY LEGAL. Obtain necessary permits or permissions. Carefully read all contracts before you sign them. If you have a church member who is an attorney, and he or she is willing, let that person read any contracts or documents first. If there is not an attorney in your congregation, find and utilize other available legal assistance. But above all, thoroughly check out liability insurance requirements with a legal advisor.

CALCULATE YOUR COSTS IN ADVANCE. Often overlooked is the cost of putting together a fundraiser. Calculate costs ahead of time to make sure you have the necessary start-up funds. Consider ways in which to obtain supplies and other resources at a discount, or even as a donation. Many business people are more than willing to help; you need only to ask.

KEEP GOOD RECORDS. Accurate records of what you do in regard to your first fund-raiser will help you duplicate and improve upon your success. Records help in the evaluation of your events. A well-documented event now is easier to plan and promote in future years!

TIME YOUR EVENT WISELY. Check with church, school, and other appropriate calendars before setting a date for your event. You would not want to run your fundraiser against the big football game! Avoid dates such as special holidays (unless your fundraiser is linked with the holiday) and avoid April, if at all possible, because of tax season. Also, check with other large churches and organizations regarding the dates of their fundraisers if you feel yours might compete with theirs. Also, check with your volunteer workers so as not to place something on the calendar that creates a conflict with their schedules.

EVALUATE YOUR FUNDRAISER. Evaluate your efforts with your planning team as soon after the event as possible. The time will be well spent. (Hint: People will evaluate more enthusiastically if food, fun, and appreciation are part of the process.)

As part of evaluating, look at more than just dollars collected. Was the energy devoted to the effort worth the dollars collected? Analyze also the effect the fundraiser had on group morale. Ask your planning team what they would do differently if they had it to do over.

SAY THANK YOU
Failure to promptly acknowledge those who have given to our fundraisers is the most critical mistake we make in our fundraising efforts. When it

takes weeks or months to acknowledge gifts, or when we fail to recognize donations at all, we are not modeling Christian gratitude, and we are not holding ourselves accountable. We are missing out on opportunities for ministry, and laying the groundwork for future fundraising failure.

By immediately following up through personalized thank-you letters (to individuals, in the church bulletin, open letters of appreciation in our organization's newsletter—whatever combinations of gestures that appropriately thank the givers for their gifts), we will be demonstrating an attitude of gratitude. Thanking those who give to our work demonstrates our willingness to be held accountable for how the money is spent. Periodic updates provide givers with a picture of how their resources are being used.

When donors give, they are making a statement—they have a desire to affiliate with your cause; they wish to see the Gospel reach more young people; they have a desire to give back to God. However, someone may have donated to receive personal satisfaction, or perhaps he or she felt obligated to help others. Whatever the reason, we need to respond to their giving. Follow up, in some way, with all donors! You will find a number of follow-up ideas in Chapter Fifteen.

CHAPTER TWO

LET'S TALK ETHICS!

CHRISTIAN FUNDRAISING HAS TAKEN IT ON THE CHIN because of the highly questionable fundraising techniques and mismanagement of funds that have been uncovered in some well-known and highly visible Christian organizations.

Wesley Willmer, who at the time of his writing was the director of development at Wheaton College, points out that how we raise money is more important than how much we raise. We need to move away from the "if it works, do it" philosophy so common among those who raise funds today. Willmer provides a godly perspective that is applicable not only to the full-time professional fundraiser for whom he writes, but also for youth workers ministering in and out of church settings. His comments were published in *Fundraising Management* (July 1987), in which Willmer points out that our Judeo-Christian faith and tradition need to guide our efforts—sixteen of Christ's thirty-eight parables and one in every six verses of Scripture deal with how our possessions ought to be handled. These biblical principles ought to govern our fundraising whether we are seeking donations from inside or outside the church, whether or not those we are asking for funds are Christians, and whether our youth-serving organization is Christian or secular. The following principles are based on his writing.

First, Willmer believes we need to emphasize the fact that *the money we are raising already belongs to God.* When we ask for money, we are not asking donors for *their* money, but *God's* money. When we raise funds, we provide the opportunity for people to be good stewards of the money that God has given to them. This means that we, too, must be good stewards of the money we raise. All resources belong to God and are not to be wasted.

Second, Willmer points out that *people are more important than the money they give.* The Bible clearly teaches that all are created in God's image. People are important to God, be they Christians or atheists. All have value. For the Christian fundraiser, this translates into caring about the spiritual life of those who give. When people give, they also offer us an opportunity to talk with them about what they value, what is important to them, and about their spiritual condition. Fundraising for the Christian is more than getting the donation; it includes ministering to the giver.

Third, we are encouraged by Willmer to *maintain a responsible balance between work and prayer in our fundraising efforts.* If our work is God's work, then we can rely on him to provide the resources. This however, does not absolve us of our responsibility to work hard. Willmer uses the story of Nehemiah (Neh. 4) to illustrate this balance. Nehemiah was confident that God would provide protection to those who were working to rebuild the wall around Jerusalem. His reliance on God is unquestioned, yet he did not neglect to post half of his workers around the perimeter of the city to guard the other half while they worked.

Fourth, Willmer notes that *we are God's fundraisers.* We belong to him, and we need to cultivate the relationship we have with him so that it will grow.

Our commitment to Jesus Christ is an example not only to those on our fundraising team, but to the donor as well.

We are God's fundraisers, raising God's money from God's people for God's work! With these truths in mind, let's examine seven biblical principles of fundraising that Willmer offers us:

WORK WITHIN EXISTING RELATIONSHIPS. Biblical examples of fundraising take place within the framework of already existing relationships. The New Testament as well as the Old places an emphasis upon relationships. Moses was asked by God to raise funds to build a tabernacle, a sanctuary where God would dwell among his people. And Moses was asked to raise the funds from the Israelites (Exod. 25:1–9). Paul raised funds by going to those in "partnership" with him (Phil. 1:5), his "loyal yokefellow" (Phil. 4:3). The best place for us to look when in need of funds is those we already have a relationship with, who understand what we are trying to do with young people.

EMPHASIZE OPPORTUNITY, NOT JUST NEED. We do not need to beg for money! "We can't make it without your donation." "If you don't give, this kid may not find Christ." Paul never resorts to this sort of begging. He appeals to the fact that all the resources people possess were first God's resources. Giving, then, is an opportunity to be good stewards of those God-owned and -given resources (Phil. 4:10–13).

SEEK INVOLVEMENT AND COMMITMENT. Our emphasis needs to be on loyal and committed involvement rather than on token donations. We will want to nurture relationships of mutual support that tie givers into our organization's cause. Our donors desire to have ownership in what we seek to accomplish with their gift. Paul states that his Philippian supporters "sent me aid again and again when I was in need" (Phil. 4:16).

REALIZE THE GIVER IS MORE IMPORTANT THAN THE GIFT. Be servants, not manipulators. Undue pressure, guilt, and scare tactics—are all fundraising methods that should be rejected by Christians.

RECOGNIZE THAT THERE WILL BE SPIRITUAL BLESSING. When we raise funds for youth work, we are offering opportunities for people to invest in what God is doing. And givers will receive a spiritual investment when they participate (Phil. 4:17). We are doing more than collecting money. We are providing the opportunity for people to share in what we are doing. Any fundraising endeavor must offer opportunities for donors to further invest their resources in our cause, as well as ways they can keep abreast of how their money is being used.

REALIZE THAT DONORS ARE GIVING UP A PIECE OF THEIR TREASURE. Willmer points out that the difficulty in giving is getting that first gift. Once that has been given, those who are raising funds must view that gift as a piece of the giver's heart. The Bible teaches that where people invest their treasure offers clues to their priorities (Matt. 6:21). When an investment is made in your youth work, it should be taken seriously. People are demonstrating that they believe in what you are doing. Acknowledge this investment and treat it carefully.

KNOW WHY THE DONOR GIVES. This principle is imperative for long-term fundraising. The more you know about your givers, the better your planning will be (Prov. 24:3–4).

> Never exploit sacred trust, manipulate a person,
> hide costs, or avoid reporting failures.

Our efforts need to be up-front and forthright. We are accountable to God and to those who have invested in our youth work. Smother your fundraising campaigns with prayer. It is not your work but God's.

SECTION Two

OVER 150
MONEY-MAKING IDEAS

CHAPTER THREE

SIX QUICK & EASY WAYS TO MAKE AT LEAST $1,000

WE HAVE COLLECTED SIX EASY-TO-DO FUNDRAISERS that, if done correctly, can net almost any group at least one thousand dollars. While most of the fundraisers in this book fall into this category, we have selected these six because they are relatively quick and easy. They may or may not work in your situation. Consider them as you put together a fundraising package to finance your next retreat, mission trip or service project.

FUNDRAISING EXEMPTION INSURANCE

Create wallet-sized "Fundraising Exemption Insurance Cards" (see sample on page 30). Photocopy these on thick, colored paper. This "insurance card" guarantees the authorized card holder comprehensive protection against being asked by your group for funds for one year. You must be able to back this up! So make the cards available in large amounts, perhaps twenty, fifty, one hundred dollars, or more.

You can also create a one-page "Insurance Policy" that outlines your group's cause and the terms and conditions of the protection policy (see page 31). There can be a place for purchasers to sign at the bottom.

FIRST CHURCH YOUTH GROUP
FUNDRAISING EXEMPTION INSURANCE CARD

Guaranteeing Comprehensive Protection Against
Fundraising Projects for One Year

_____
AUTHORIZED SIGNATURE

This card entitles the authorized user to protection for one full year (_____ to _____) from participation in any First Church youth group car washes, banquets, golf tournaments, auctions, fun runs, candy sales, contests, or other fundraising efforts.

The holder of this card, by retaining and using it, agrees to the terms and conditions under which it has been issued.

This card can also be used as a $10,000 bail bond if any court will accept it!

If you lose your card or your address changes, please report it immediately and we will sell you a new card at a discounted price.

Proceeds from the sale of this card will be used to support the First Church youth group's summer work camp.

DOOR-TO-DOOR PENNY DRIVE

You can go door-to-door in neighborhoods collecting pennies with great success. We recommend, however, that you visit only the homes of people known by group members.

Here's how it works. Make up some large name tags that identify your group and its purpose. Require group members to travel in groups of three or more people.

The teams can visit the neighborhoods of group members, knocking on the doors of the neighbors and friends of your group members. Give each team a hand dolly with a five-gallon plastic bottled water bottle secured to the hand dolly with a bungee cord or rope. The water bottles may be donated from a water supply store or purchased wholesale. (Investing in a

INSURANCE POLICY

This fundraising protection policy guarantees to the authorized policy holder comprehensive protection from obligations to contribute to any First Church youth group fundraising projects for one year, including:

BAKE SALES	CAR WASHES
BANQUETS	AUCTIONS
FUN RUNS	GOLF TOURNAMENTS
CANDY SALES	CONTESTS

All money raised from the sale of said policies will go to our summer work camp. Our youth group is traveling to the Navajo Indian Reservation in Sedalia, Arizona, to work with Native American children. We will be working with a Navajo church conducting a Vacation Bible School, coaching the children in sports, organizing basketball and soccer tournaments, operating a community carnival, assisting with church services, planting trees and building a playground.

If you would like to make an additional donation, please contact the church office at 555-3234. Thanks for your support!

This insurance goes into effect at 12:01 A.M., Standard Time on _____ and will terminate at 12:01 A.M., Standard Time on _____.

_____
AUTHORIZED POLICY-HOLDER SIGNATURE

_____
OFFICIAL YOUTH GROUP MEMBER SIGNATURE

number of them pays off in the long run, because they can be used again and again.) It also pays to place a plastic funnel into the bottle (car radiator funnel) that has a spout big enough for pennies, nickels and dimes. These funnels become a slide for the coins. The faster people can pour coins into your bottle, the more money they will deposit. Teams go from house to house, asking occupants to contribute to your cause. Most people gladly donate because you are asking for only a handful of pennies. If people ask, you may also accept nickels, dimes, quarters and dollar bills (with two forms of ID!).

THE ALL-YOU-CAN'T-EAT FUNDRAISING DINNER

You can sponsor a successful money-making dinner by not holding one at all. That's right! Ask people to contribute a set amount for the dinner, but tell them they don't have to bother attending. Because there is no dinner and donors know this, you are freed from the organizational hassle of putting together a successful dinner or banquet. The only work you need to do is sell tickets, which you would have had to do anyway if you actually held the dinner.

You can finance a complete retreat, for example, if each young person who wants to attend sells enough tickets to pay his or her way. For example, if your

---

BACK BY POPULAR DEMAND

THE SECOND ANNUAL FIRST CHURCH

ALL YOU CAN'T EAT DINNER

The dinner will NOT be held on May 32

Tickets now on sale for only $5.00. All proceeds go to the youth ministry winter retreat fund!

winter retreat will cost seventy-five dollars per person and your tickets to your non-event sell for five dollars, each retreat participant can pay his or her way by selling fifteen tickets.

You can create a ribbon memento of the non-event by using thicker stock paper on your church or organization photocopy machine. Every one who purchases a ticket gets a ribbon. Ribbons help people remember the all-you-can't-eat dinner and why they gave to it.

HONORABLE
MENTION

Amy Ferguson
didn't make a
pig of herself

at the Second Annual
First Church

ALL YOU
CAN'T EAT
DINNER

HONORABLE
MENTION

John Ferguson
didn't make a
pig of himself

at the Second Annual
First Church

ALL YOU
CAN'T EAT
DINNER

MILES FOR MISSIONS

Planning a mission trip or work camp? Raise the needed cash by selling people the mileage of the trip. Figure out how much your trip will cost and divide that by the number of miles it takes to get to your mission's destination and back. You now have your cost per mile. People then can fund a mile or more of your trip.

Let's assume your group is traveling 1300 miles round trip. If your group needs $10,000 for the trip, you could request an eight-dollars-per-mile donation. Fully funded, this would net your group $10,400. People could purchase a quarter mile of your trip for two dollars, a half mile for four dollars and three quarters of a mile for six dollars.

You can chart your fundraising progress with a map of your round-trip route. As your group raises money, you can draw with a red marker the fundraising "road" to your destination and back again, mile after mile. Everyone will have fun watching the road being funded to your destination and back.

SKIP A MOVIE FOR MISSIONS

Calculate how much an evening at the movies would cost, on the average, in your community. Then put together a campaign to collect this amount from contributors to your next mission trip project. Your group can write and practice on each other a presentation that outlines your mission project before you take your fundraiser on the road. Here is a sample presentation.

> Hi, my name is John. I am with the youth group at First Church. We have planned a summer mission trip to Mexico, where we will be refurbishing an orphanage as well as conducting a children's Bible school. You can participate with us in this project by donating what it would cost you to attend one movie per month this summer. We figure that the average family of four will spend forty dollars including popcorn, candy, and sodas. Our youth group has surveyed the upcoming summer movie pickings and have declared it to be a "bummer summer." We don't want to see you waste your hard-earned money on a worthless movie. Your can rest assured that your movie money will not be wasted on our mission trip.

BULLISH ON THE YOUTH GROUP

Here's a creative way to finance your next mission trip or service project. Print up stock certificates and sell them to members of the church or community as an "investment." Each share can sell for a set amount—say five dollars—with no limit on how many shares a person can buy.

The purchasers own "stock" in the project which entitles them to attend a "stockholders meeting" where they can be informed as to how their investment is doing (you can include singing, testimonies and other worship activities). A "stockholders report" can also be printed. The "dividends" they receive are the results of the work completed by the youth group. It is probably a good idea to have a meeting before the trip and one after. Both the meeting and the report can include photos, testimonies by the kids who participated, a financial statement, and so on. "Stockholders" will appreciate learning about the "dividends"—the results of the work.

This idea will work. Bank on it!

CHAPTER FOUR

GIVING PROMPTERS

GIVING PROMPTERS ARE TOOLS THAT YOU CAN USE to present a case for donating to your group's cause. Identify those that will work with your group, modify them to fit your needs, and you have a creative way to ask people to donate.

BUCK-A-ROO CLUB

To raise money for an upcoming camp, retreat, or other activity, sign up members of the congregation to join the Buck-a-Roo Club. Members donate one dollar for each youth participating in a given event. For example, if fifteen young people are going to the youth convention, each Buck-a-Roo Clubber would donate fifteen dollars. It's simple and relatively inexpensive for each donor. Acknowledge the givers with Buck-a-Roo Club membership cards.

CALENDAR PAY-OFF

Here's an idea that encourages your kids to be givers. Print up a calendar that has a space for each day of the month. In each space, enter an instruction that will determine how much money they must give that day. The instructions should be humorous, and amounts to be given should vary from day to day. When the month is up, the kids bring in the money they owe.

You can vary this by printing the instruction for each day on separate slips of paper, then fold them and staple them to your calendar, so that they are concealed until the end of each day. The instruction can then be a "fine" for certain things done or not done. For example, one might say, "Pay fifty cents for each class you were late to today," or, "Pay twenty-five cents if you forgot to brush your teeth." Allow a space on the calendar where kids can write in how much they owe each day. You might add one "extra" space for them to give any amount they choose. They can total these amounts up at the end of the month. This approach adds a little fun and variety to giving.

COUPON DOLLARS WEEK

Declare a certain week of the year as "Coupons for Camp" or "Coupons for Missions Week." During this week, all participants pledge to contribute to your project all the money they save that week with grocery coupons. Consider including rebates and refunds as well. Participants redeem their coupons, rebates and refunds during your coupon week and donate what they saved to your youth group cause.

You can solicit participants in advance by passing out pledge cards that announce the dates for your coupon week, and the cause to which the proceeds are going.

DOLLAR FOR DOLLAR

One creative way to raise funds easily is by asking your church's mission committee to match what your youth group raises for a mission trip, dollar for dollar. Para-church youth groups can also approach their local committees with the same challenge. Mission committees are often more willing to give money when their contribution is matched by your group.

FREE CAR WASH

Set up a youth-sponsored car wash at a local shopping center or filling station as you normally would. However, instead of charging for the wash tickets, give them away. Advertise it as a "FREE CAR WASH." Make it clear that there are no strings attached. Anyone may get their car washed free by the youth of your church as a gesture of Christian love and friendship. Those who wish to make a contribution can do so, in any amount they choose. Post a sign at the car wash site similar to this one:

> Your car is being washed by the youth of First Church. This is a free service with no strings attached. It's a small way for us to demonstrate to you the love of Jesus Christ.
>
> Another way we are attempting to share Christ's love is by collecting funds to help purchase food for the hungry. If you would like to help us with this project, your contribution would be greatly appreciated. Thank you and God bless you.

Print this information on your tickets as well. One youth group did this twice and raised a total of $800. Pick a good (busy) location, make sure you have plenty of hardworking, friendly young people, and the experience can be very rewarding.

"HOW NOT TO RAISE SUPPORT" SKIT

Try this great skit next time you ask the congregation to contribute to the church's youth ministry.

"How Not to Raise Support" Cast:

Man (or woman)
Operator (offstage; voice over the P.A. system)
Salesperson
Actor 1 (light bulb seller)
Actor 2 (con artist)
Actor 3 (TP-marathon contestant)
Actor 4 (beggar)
Actor 5 (woman who drops the dollar)
Actor 6 (whiner)

Open with a man dialing a phone *(ringing heard offstage)*. An operator answers:

Operator: *(Offstage; voice is heard over the P.A. system)* Acme Fundraising. Can I help you?

Man: Well, I hope so. You see, I'm planning to go on a mission trip this summer and I'm having a little problem with raising money. I need some help.

Operator: Oh, I'm sure we can solve your problem. I'll send someone right over.

Man: Thanks. I appreciate it. *(Before he hangs up, there is a knock at the door. The man opens the door and finds a boisterous, grinning salesperson.)*

Salesperson: Hi! I'm from Acme Fundraising, here to help you get the financial backing you so richly deserve!

Man: Oh, I—

Salesperson: Now don't worry about a thing! We'll get money from everyone you know and even some people you don't know! I have this pamphlet here entitled "Five Easy Ways to Raise Money," which I would like to share with you. Let me describe, with the assistance of my assistants, our five guaranteed-to-get-results fundraising methods that we know will work for you! *(Hands the man a pamphlet.)*

Man: I don't know—

Salesperson: Number one—turn to page two there, son—Number one: the first way to raise money is to take a cheap item and sell it for a huge profit. People will buy it from you—even if they don't need it, or can get it cheaper somewhere else—just to get rid of you! Watch what I mean.

(Actor 1 approaches Man.)

Actor 1: Excuse me, sir, but would you like to buy one or more of my special high-quality, glow-in-the-dark light bulbs? I have here a powerful *(here he mumbles something unintelligible)* -watt bulb guaranteed to light up your life for years and years—*(in a stage whisper)* or until I leave—and the cost is only $12.95, postage and handling included. And all the proceeds go to feed hungry children.

Man: I don't know . . . that looks like a thirty-cent light bulb to—

Salesperson: No matter. It works. It sells. It raises money! But then, not everyone needs a light bulb. So here's method number two: Lucky Lotto!

Man: What?

Salesperson: It's like playing the lottery! People put down a dollar and have a chance to win a bundle. It plays to people's basic nature—greed and avarice, to be precise. It's wonderful! Here's how it works.

(Actor 2 approaches Man.)

Actor 2: *(Dressed like game-show host)* Hey, here's your chance to help a worthy cause and help yourself even more! Just buy a few of these lucky raffle tickets and you, yes you, could be the lucky winner of a brand new BMW convertible, a trip to Hawaii, and a year's supply of glow-in-the-dark lightbulbs! How many would you like?

Man: I'm really not sure I—

Salesperson: It works! And that's what's important—the bottom line.

Man: Sure . . . uh, what's method number three?

Salesperson: I'm glad you asked that question. Method number three is the "Give-a-thon." Take pledges for some ridiculous thing you're doing—the crazier it is, the more money people will give to it. It works like a charm.

(Actor 3 approaches Man.)

Actor 3: Hi, I'm taking pledges for our TP-a-thon. Next Saturday our youth group is going to TP houses all over the city. Would you donate a dollar for every house we completely cover with toilet paper?

Man: Wha—?

Salesperson: Hey, one youth group TP'd 7,000 houses in one day and put half the town in debt to them. Some people had to mortgage their houses to pay off. It's a winner of an idea, I'm telling you that.

Man: Any other ideas?

Salesperson: Method number four is this: beg.

Man: Beg?

Salesperson: It's biblical. And it's proven. One of the oldest methods around.

(Actors 4 and 5 enter stage. Actor 4, sitting, wearing dark glasses, appears to be blind, holding a tin cup. Actor 5 walks by and, intending to drop a dollar bill in the cup, misses. The "blind" beggar lowers his glasses some, sees the bill on the ground, and grabs it.)

Man: Hey, you can't raise money for the Lord's work like that!

Salesperson: Look, here's one more way. This one always works, but it takes training and persistence. It's the guilt-trip method. The idea is for you to make people feel guilty for not giving you what you want. No one wants to feel guilty—and the best way to get rid of guilt is to get rid of you by giving you what you want! It's foolproof!

(Actor 6 approaches Man.)

Actor 6: *(Whining)* Dad! Don't you care what could happen to me if I don't go on this trip? I could miss the challenge that God has prepared for me. And if I miss that challenge, I might become depressed and discouraged, which might lead me to worldly pleasures—sex, drugs, rock'n'roll. I might become an axe-murderer, a street-corner wino, a bag lady . . . yes, I can see it now—

Man: Stop! I've had enough! Get out! I'll just have to find some way to raise money on my own!

Salesperson: (*Leaving*) Well, good luck. You really think you can rely on God's people to just give willingly—from their heart or something? Nobody gives like that anymore. People need gimmicks—and so do you. Here's my card—call me if you change your mind. (*Exits, leaving man alone on stage. He now addresses the audience, presenting the need to the congregation and asking them if they would be willing to give from their hearts.*)

IRONMAN CONTEST

Select some willing men (church board and staff members, dads, and the like) to compete in this hilarious fundraiser which can be held following an evening service. The contestants, armed with their own iron, board, and shirts, will iron as many shirts as possible in a given amount of time. Each shirt is judged for quality and detail while people in the audience pledge money to any or all of the "Ironmen" for each shirt completed. A trophy is presented to the best overall Ironman, with certificates going to all contestants. Money is collected at a designated table before people leave.

PROMOTION. A few weeks before the contest, present a skit to the congregation, playing off the idea of the Ironman Triathlon. (See *Ironman Promotional Dialogue* on page 45–46.) One week before the contest, invite one of the contestants who is claiming to be the shoo-in winner to the front and have him show off a shirt he has been "practicing" on. It should be burned clear through in places and scorched in others. Line up several of the best cooks to make their favorite dessert to bring the night of the contest. Have the youth group provide drinks for everyone. Don't forget to promote the food—you'll attract a larger crowd.

THE TROPHY. Make an Ironman trophy. At any trophy shop, purchase a marble base with an undated brass plate engraved with "Ironman Champion," then find an old travel iron at a thrift shop, spray it with gold paint, and mount it on the base. You can circulate the trophy in subsequent Ironman fundraisers.

THE PLEDGES. You can receive pledges the night of the contest, which saves time and requires less planning, or you can display pictures of the contestant in a high traffic area of your church and let your kids collect pledges like other "a-thons" for any or all of the Ironmen. (See Ironman Pledge Sheet on page 47).

THE BIG DAY. Set up the contest like a TV game show. Ask someone to keep a running commentary on the contestants during the action. (If possible, pick someone who has a sense of humor so that the commentary is funny and fast-paced.) Use a portable scoreboard clock or videotape a scoreboard/ swimming clock and play the tape to show the time elapsed. Play some fast-paced game-show-type music to intensify the contest. The wives of each contestant can act as personal trainers and coaches. Give them water bottles and sweat rags and let them play their part to the hilt.

JUDGING. Make copies of the Ironman Contest Judging Form on page 46 for judges to use in determining the winner of the contest. Check for things like creases on the sleeves, wrinkles in the collar, smoothness around the buttons, pleats in the back, overall crispness of the shirt, whether an apron was worn, whether the wife helped. Each area can be rated from one to ten.

THE CONSPIRACY. Midway through the contest, draw the audience's attention to the fact that the trophy is missing and accuse one of the contestants of stealing the trophy and selling it. Then play a hidden camera video (like FBI footage) of two unidentifiable people in a motel room exchanging the trophy for a large sum of money.

Presentation is everything for the Ironman Contest to be successful. Make it as fun as possible for the audience as well as the contestants. Have plenty of pledge sheets on hand so that everyone present can get in on the fun.

Ironman Promotional Dialogue

Perform this promotional skit to your congregation a week or two before the Ironman Contest. Equip someone with a ridiculous amount of athletic gear—a bike, biker's helmet, running shoes, Lycra tights, stopwatch, and so on. Throw in a snorkel and mask and a backpack.

Person is already in the auditorium. The Ironman enters.

Person: *(as if the Ironman is interrupting)* Excuse me!

Ironman: Yes?

Person: Who are you?

Ironman: I'm Biff.

Person: And what are you doing, Biff?

Ironman: Radical mind twister, dude. I'm training.

Person: Training for what?

Ironman: The greatest test of man's endurance, agility, and strength.

Person: And what might that be?

Ironman: The Ironman Contest, man. See my equipment? *(Shows it off.)*

Person: Yeah . . . that's, uh, impressive, but isn't the Ironman Triathlon in Hawaii?

Ironman: No, man. I just saw posters up everywhere saying there was going to be an Ironman Contest here.

Person: Well, yes. We are having an Ironman Contest, but it's not the same kind of Ironman Contest.

Ironman: Huh?

Person: Would you like to see the trophy? *(Holds up trophy of an iron—as in "ironing board.")*

Ironman: Dude! That's an iron!

Person: Very perceptive! Our Ironman Contest will decide which of our iron-men from our church board are the best at PRESSING toward their goal of being the best at handling an iron. The contest is to help raise money for the youth group here at *(name of your church)*.

Ironman: Totally excellent! But what about food? I'm not coming unless there's food.

Person: We'll have some of the best desserts that you'll find anywhere. It all happens here *(date and time)* after the evening service, so don't miss it.

IRONMAN CONTEST JUDGING FORM

for _____

Rate each category on a scale from 1 to 10

_____	Completed shirt	1 to 10 points
_____	Wore apron	1 to 10 points
_____	Creases on sleeves	1 to 10 points
_____	Collar	1 to 10 points
_____	Button front	1 to 10 points
_____	Overall crispness of shirt	1 to 10 points
_____	No help from wife	1 to 10 points
_____	**TOTAL POINTS**	

IRONMAN PLEDGE SHEET

Name _____

Address _____

City/State/Zip _____

Phone (_____) _____

Please fill out your pledge by indicating which Ironman you would like to pledge toward. (1) Write in the amount you want to pledge per shirt. (2) When the contest is finished, calculate what the total is for each Ironman. (3) Add up your total for all pledges taken. (4) When you have completed your form, take it to the designated table where you can arrange for payment. (5) The stub at the bottom of this form can be used as your receipt.

IRONMAN	PLEDGE PER SHIRT	NUMBER OF SHIRTS	TOTAL PLEDGED
_____	$ _____	x _____	= $ _____
_____	$ _____	x _____	= $ _____
_____	$ _____	x _____	= $ _____
_____	$ _____	x _____	= $ _____
_____	$ _____	x _____	= $ _____
_____	$ _____	x _____	= $ _____

Grand Total: $ _____

Thank you for your continuing support for the youth group of our church.

....

IRONMAN CONTEST

Date _____ Total: $ _____

Thank you for your support!

IRONMAN CONTEST

This is to certify that

_____

participated in the

19_____ **IRONMAN CONTEST**

and has received the

_____

award on this

_____ day of _____ , 19_____

THE PINK FLAMINGO

Purchase several of those tacky plastic pink flamingos that people put in their yards. Send everyone an announcement (on pink paper, of course) with the following information about your Pink Flamingo fundraiser. The number of "flamingo areas" will vary with the size of your congregation or organization and the number of available flamingos.

A pink flamingo may be coming to your house! On May 22 the youth group of First Church will conduct its first annual

Pink Flamingo Fundraiser

We have several lovely pink flamingos, one of which may end up in your front yard.

We have divided the congregation into four Flamingo Areas. Inside each pink flamingo is a list of the names and addresses of church members living in one of the Flamingo Areas.

On the appointed day, the youth group will plant each of the flamingos in the front yard of one family from the Flamingo List. If the flamingo ends up in your front yard, you then—

- Pledge a free-will donation to the youth group.
- Cross your name off the Flamingo List.
- Replant the flamingo in the yard of someone whose name has not yet been crossed off your list.

The flamingo may not remain in the same yard for more than twenty-four hours. You need not pass the flamingo in the order of the listed names. Your free-will donations may be placed in the pink flamingo located in the lobby of the church sanctuary. Do not put your offering in the flamingo that you deliver to the next house. Make checks payable to First Church Youth Ministry.

"But wait," you say. "I don't want to wake up to a pink flamingo in my front yard." Then you'll want to purchase Anti-Pink-Flamingo Insurance for only ten dollars (an application for insurance is enclosed). If you carry Anti-Pink-Flamingo Insurance, your property is guaranteed to be designated a "Flamingo-Free Zone." Purchase deadline is May 15.

Anti-Pink-Flamingo Insurance

PINK Cross PINK Shield Insurance Company
5601 Flamingo Drive ■ Sioux City, IA 51106
AGENT: Middle School Youth Group ■ First Church Sioux City, IA 51106

Name of Insured _____

Insured Location (Flamingo Area) _____

Street Address _____

City/State/Zip _____

Policy Period: From May 22 through the duration of the First
Church Middle School Youth Group Pink Flamingo Fundraiser.
Effective: 12:00 P.M. May 22

We will provide the insurance described in this policy in return for
the premium and compliance with all applicable policy provisions.

A. This policy constitutes an agreement between the named insured
and the First Church Middle School Youth Group backed by the
PINK Cross PINK Shield Insurance Company.

B. This policy provides that we (First Church Middle School Youth
Group) will not place or request someone else to place the hideous
Pink Flamingo at the above location.

Exclusions: If someone puts The Pink Flamingo on your lawn anyway, hey, what can we do?

This supersedes all previous declarations, states your current coverage, and represents the terms and conditions of this contract.

INSURANCE PREMIUM TOTAL $10.00

Countersigned by _____ Date _____
                  FIRST CHURCH MIDDLE SCHOOL YOUTH GROUP

Insured Signature _____ Date _____

KIDNAP THE PASTOR

Have the group "kidnap" the pastor and other well-known individuals in the church (prearranged, of course!) with the ransom being a set amount of money to be used for a youth project. This works best if done on a Saturday. Young people telephone people in the congregation informing them of the kidnappings and the ransom amount required. Church members can pledge a dollar amount to be given on Sunday morning. If the ransom isn't paid up, the youth should be prepared to handle the morning service or the responsibilities of the other kidnapped individuals. Your group will have a ball being creative with this one.

PROJECT PARTNERS

When your group wants to finance a specific outreach project, you can ask individuals to become Project Partners. Young people find project sponsors willing to partially finance the project. In return for their sponsorship, the partners are given reports by the young people whom they are backing financially. For example, if your group has planned a mission trip to Jamaica, each of your young people should write a letter a week to their sponsors keeping them abreast of the project's progress. Before the trip, host a breakfast or lunch for the sponsors at which the young people report on the goals of the project. Upon your return, hold a follow-up "thank you" dessert party for your Project Partners, updating them on what happened during the trip.

SPOOK INSURANCE

Sell "insurance policies" (see sample on page 52) at Halloween to families in the church promising the young people will provide cleanup services in the event that protected households are subjected to any of the usual pranks that go along with the ghoulish holiday. Triple the price for businesses. Since most of your policy holders will not need cleanup services, it is clear profit. Make sure your kids are committed to do the work in case it is needed.

Spook Insurance

Policy 1: This policy protects your lawn against such disasters as being strewn with candy wrappers, rotten eggs, water balloon scraps, T.P. (toilet paper), etc.

Policy 2: This policy protects your windows against graffiti, wax, soap, eggs, and other foreign materials. (Does not cover breakage!)

Please fill out the following information:

Name _____

Address _____

City/State/Zip _____

Phone (_____) _____

Check one of the following.
- ☐ Policy 1: Lawn mess ....Price: **$5.00**
- ☐ Policy 2: Window mess............................Price: **$5.00**
- ☐ Policy 3: 1 and 2 ....Price: **$10.00**

Please report claims to the church
before 9:00 P.M. on Wednesday, November 2.

YOUTH MINISTRY GIFT CERTIFICATES

Events cost money. So to ease the demand on parents for cash, offer gift certificates. Friends, relatives, and neighbors can buy them for birthdays, good grades, etc. The youth office or church office keeps the records. The kids (or their parents) then have to come up with less out-of-pocket cash when an event arrives.

These can also be sold to provide "scholarships" to those unable to afford youth events.

CONGRATULATIONS!
They say it's your birthday.

Happy Birthday

Youth Ministry Gift Certificate

This Youth Ministry Gift Certificate for

_____

signifies that _____ dollars have been
given in your name for your involvement
in an upcoming youth event.

Happy,
Valentine's Day

This Youth Ministry Gift Certificate for

_____

signifies that _____ dollars have been
given in your name for your involvement
in an upcoming youth event.
You are loved! Congratulations!

Merry Christmas

Youth Ministry Gift Certificate

This Youth Ministry Gift Certificate for

_____

signifies that _____ dollars have been
given in your name for your involvement
in an upcoming youth event.
You are loved! Merry Christmas!

YOUTH MINISTRY
Gift Certificate

This Youth Ministry Gift Certificate for

_____

signifies that _____ dollars have been
given in your name for your involvement
in an upcoming youth event.

CONGRATULATIONS!

CHAPTER FIVE

FOOD 'N' FUN

THERE'S ONE THING YOU CAN COUNT ON PEOPLE DOING AND THAT'S EATING. And that habit can help you raise money. The ideas presented here all focus on money making opportunities that involve food. You can maximize your fundraising profits with these ideas when you are able to get food items donated.

You can also educate your group about hunger and poverty with selected food fundraisers.

AFTER-CHURCH SALAD BAR

Many church youth groups provide coffee and donuts for the church after the morning worship service (see Donut Delight, page 58). A great variation of this is to provide a salad bar instead. It's easy to do and the adults love it. Have the youth purchase and prepare all the ingredients—lettuce, tomatoes, mushrooms, sprouts, sunflower seeds, salad dressings, etc.—and set it up in the fellowship area after the service. People who participate can pay a set price for the salad bar or make a contribution of any amount to the youth group.

ALTERNATIVE DINING

This fundraiser has generated hundreds of dollars for youth groups and it's a people pleaser, too. Simply fix dinner for the congregation after the morning church service. Keep it simple—sloppy joes or spaghetti for the main dish, carrot and celery sticks (Note: Toddlers choke on these.) or deli salads, chips, cookies. And you can bill it as "Alternative Dining: No cooking, no mess, no fast food, no cold pizza, no long lines."

The people can wander in whenever they have finished visiting after the service and can leave whenever they want. There are no tickets either— just a donation box at the door. (Don't worry! Youth groups from modest sized churches have raised at least two to three hundred dollars profit per meal.) Just keep the line moving and bring seconds to the tables for those requesting them. Senior highers can cook, set up, clean up, serve, and act as hosts and hostesses. Once you serve the people in you church like this, they may demand alternative dining every month!

BAGEL BREAKFAST

Preparing and delivering pre-sold bagel breakfasts requires some legwork, but the fun and profit to your youth group make it worthwhile.

Choose a Sunday for delivering the breakfasts. Several weeks prior to the event, get your kids together to plan a breakfast menu. An easy meal could include one quart of milk, one quart of orange juice, four croissants and four bagels, and a copy of the morning paper of your choice. (Ask the newspaper for free copies for the day of your event.) Create a logo expressing the purpose of the fundraiser, then duplicate it and glue the logos on the grocery sacks in which you'll deliver the breakfast. Schedule announcement dates and opportunities to pre-sell the breakfasts to members of the congregation, as well as friends and neighbors.

Set a cost for the meal (the cost for the above meal, for example, could be fifteen dollars). Have several kids and a sponsor approach local grocery stores to request a price break on the purchase of the milk and juice, and seek out a bakery that might do the same for the breads. When merchants discover you are attempting to raise money for neighborhood youth, they are often willing to help. The profit margin can be as high as 100% to 200%.

On the Saturday before you plan to deliver the breakfasts, meet with the kids to purchase or pick up the needed products, to decorate the delivery bags with the logo, and to assign delivery teams for the next day. A group of three to five kids per delivery area will make the job both fun and efficient.

The event may be worth repeating annually, in which case the legwork becomes easier as people know what to expect and have already helped you in the past.

BAKE-IN

Here's a good fundraiser for teens who like all-night activities. The group gathers at the church or meeting place at 10:00 P.M., possibly after a ball game or other activity, to begin preparations for the baking. All the flour, sugar, eggs, milk, and other ingredients must be available for the event. These ingredients may be purchased, but it is best to get members of your church or organization and local merchants to donate items.

Several weeks in advance, advertise the event, circulate order blanks that list the items you will be baking, and take prepaid orders. With your orders in hand, there's nothing left to do but start. Enlist a few people with baking experience to help at the Bake-In. They will help the baking go smoothly and keep all the young people busy. Deliver the items you baked during the night to the purchasers' doors, or they can pick up their orders that morning. Teens get a great deal of satisfaction from this kind of a project as they see people enjoying the fruits of their labors. They also benefit from added funds for their cause.

Items you can bake include: apple and cherry strudel, banana bread, donuts, coffee cake, cinnamon rolls, white or wheat bread, muffins, cupcakes, chocolate chip cookies, sugar cookies, banana cream pie, chocolate pie, and the like. The project will go over great if you can keep from eating what you bake before it's sold.

CARHOP GRILL OUT

Have the youth group grill hamburgers, hot dogs, etc. in the church parking lot and invite the community to come and eat at the new "restaurant." The kids serve as "carhops" and wait on people in their cars, taking their orders and bringing the food. Desserts, drinks and other items should be on the "menu" as well.

DIME-A-DIP DINNER

This is an oldie but goodie that works great and builds community as well. Put on a banquet where all food is prepared and donated by members of your group. People who attend, pay a dime for every helping, scoop of food, or piece of food they put on their plate. Everything is a dime—drinks, appetizers, a pat of margarine, a potato chip, etc. When this is used to raise funds for a worthy cause, such as a mission trip, the response is very good. A program of music, a film, a speaker, or other entertainment can help to draw a crowd or provide inspiration.

DONUT DELIGHT

Here's an easy fundraiser for the youth group. Have the group bring donuts and coffee to church and provide them each Sunday before or after the morning worship service. The donuts can be donated, bought at wholesale, or homemade. The people then buy the donuts for the going price, just enough so that the youth group can make a little on each one sold. Most people really enjoy coffee and donuts in the morning at church, and are happy to pay for them.

GRANOLA PARTY

This is a fundraiser that most people can really sink their teeth into. Get the youth group together for a "granola party" where the kids make their own special brand of granola that can be sold later. Find a good recipe—preferably one that includes lots of "good stuff" like nuts, banana chips, carob chips, coconut, grains, honey, and the like. Have the kids prepare the granola in large quantities, then bag it. Put it in decorated coffee cans, and sell it door-to-door or to friends and relatives. A variation of this would be to make and sell jam, preserves, dried fruit, or other "natural" foods. You can take orders ahead of preparation. Make extra, because people will usually want to buy more.

MACHO BAKE SALE

The bake sale has always been successful as a fundraiser, but here it is with a new twist. Get the men in the church to bake cakes, cookies, and pies. You can even make it a contest among the men—and no women may help them. A macho bake sale will be a lot of fun.

PIZZA TO GO

Many people have spent time on a Saturday in a pizza parlor. On this Saturday morning, however, you will be making pizzas instead of eating them. And you will be making money too!

Organize a pizza sale for which your group takes orders and payment in advance for your homemade pizzas. Offer discounts to those who order more than one. You can purchase your ingredients using the money collected when the orders were taken.

Then organize a homemade pizza making party. You may be able to arrange with your favorite pizza establishment to use their facility and ingredients at wholesale prices. Or you can purchase your own ingredients in bulk and use your church or school kitchen. Frozen bread dough makes an excellent pizza crust. Or if you have the facilities, make the crust from scratch. Offer only two or three toppings and measure or weigh ingredients carefully to keep costs down.

Prepare the pizzas in assembly-line fashion. The custom toppings should be done as the last step. The pizza is then placed on a cardboard base and wrapped in plastic wrap with the order form attached. (A local box company may donate the cardboard pizza circles or sell them at wholesale prices.) Deliver the uncooked fresh pizzas immediately or have people pick them up. You will need refrigerator space for pizzas not immediately delivered or picked up.

Remind the customers of the worthy cause to which the pizza profits are going and thank them for their support.

SPUD NITE

A "Spud Nite" featuring a lavish baked-potato bar makes a great fundraiser. Net profits of $500 or more have been realized by groups that conduct this easy fundraiser.

Check with a restaurant supplier in order to get the largest potatoes. Then give them to students in whose homes they will be baked. For a $4 ticket (sell tickets in advance of the event or ask for a donation) people get a potato, drink, dessert, and best of all, their choice of toppings—set out buffet-style. The more toppings, the better! Add some music to the mix—either live or taped—and you'll have a dining adventure that your church or group will beg you to repeat in a few months.

Here are the quantities you'll need:

- 215 potatoes
- 10 lbs. cheddar cheese (grated)
- l gal. salad dressing (ranch)
- 24 family-size tea bags
- 1 gal. crouton/potato topping mix
- 10 lbs. margarine spread
- 10 lbs. sour cream
- 1 lb. bacon bits
- 2 oz. freeze-dried chopped chives
- 2 cans (20 lbs.) cheese sauce
- 1 can (10 lbs.) chili
- 3 bags chili beans
- 3 lbs. frozen broccoli
- 4 cans chopped green chilis
- 9 heads lettuce
- 1 lug tomatoes
- lots of aluminum foil
- other topping ingredients (see skit)

The following skit works great for publicity. It was created to be used in a church but can easily be adapted to use elsewhere.

Spud Nite Commercial

Characters

Youth group sponsor
Youth group member

Setting

Perform during the announcement time in the worship service.

Sponsor: Say, [name of youth group member], I heard about your cool fundraiser called Spud Nite. When is that again?

Member: *(with no enthusiasm)* Oh, it's _____ [date] on _____ [day] night, from _____ to _____ [time] in the _____ [place].

Sponsor: Hey, you don't sound very excited about it. What's the problem?

Member: Well, you know we've put up with lots of our youth worker's crazy ideas, but this one is the worst. Spud Nite. That sounds like something from Idaho. I don't think many [your state] are going to come to something called Spud Nite.

Sponsor: What? Nobody come to Spud Nite? These just aren't your ordinary potatoes, bud. These baked beauties will be covered with your choice of any delicious toppings like nacho cheese, cheddar cheese, chili, salsa, ham, broccoli, mushrooms, sour cream, butter, bacon, hamburger, or onions. These aren't common tators, I can guarantee that. Trust me, this spud's for you. Besides, a lot of people in this church love potatoes. Why they grew up with potatoes at every meal. In fact, most of these people are part potato.

Member: What do you mean they're part potato?

Sponsor: Well, when I look over this crowd, I see all sorts of potatoes.

Member: You do?

Sponsor: Sure. Look at that guy back there. See him? His name is Dick Tator. He'll *tell* his wife to take a night off and go to Spud Nite.

Member: Really?

Sponsor: Yeah. And look over there. See that guy? His name is Commen Tator. He's always got something to say. He'll be there because he will want something to *talk* about next Sunday morning after church.

Member: Say, I think I see a tator out there.

Sponsor: Where?

Member: Look over there. See that lady? That's Hesi Tator. She's *not sure* she wants to come. What did you say would be on those potatoes at Spud Nite?

Sponsor: *(loudly)* I said, "These baked beauties will be covered with your choice of any delicious toppings like nacho cheese, cheddar cheese, chili, salsa, ham, broccoli, mushrooms, sour cream, butter, bacon, hamburger, or onions."

Member: Not so loud!

Sponsor: Why not?

Member: You'll wake up Medi Tator here in the front row.

Sponsor: Oh, sorry.

Member: You know [name of sponsor], the more I think about Spud Nite and the more I look at this great group of people here, the more I really think we will have a great turnout.

Together: (to the audience) Come out and support the [youth group name] fundraiser next week. Don't crash in front of the TV and be a Vegi Tator. Don't sit out in the parking lot and be a Spec Tator. Be an Immi Tator and follow everyone else to the [place, date and time] for a night your taste spuds will never forget!

SUPER SUNDAY SUB SALE

A couple of weeks before the Super Bowl, put a flyer in your church bulletin or organization bulletin announcing that your youth group is sponsoring a sub sale on Super Sunday. Include the price of the subs, when to pick them up (delivery service is even better), a list of fillings available and a tear-off with space for name, address, phone number, and number of subs ordered.

Check local delis or supermarkets to see if someone will sell you sub supplies at a discount. A deli owner could also help you estimate quantities of the ingredients you'll need for the number of subs ordered. The deli might even be willing to prepare the materials so that your group need only to assemble them. Besides raising money, this project builds team spirit as you work in a production line to put the subs together, package them, and deliver them. You may even want to make enough extras for a Super Bowl party of your own after you're done with cleanup and delivery.

SAMPLE SHOPPING LIST FOR 100 SUBS: 9 lbs. ham; 9 lbs. cheese; 9½ lbs. salami; 16 heads of lettuce; 5 lbs. tomatoes; 6 bottles Italian dressing; 2 bottles oregano; 3 lbs. onions; 100 sub rolls; lots of wrapping paper.

UN-DINNER FOR WORLD HUNGER

This is a good idea to help your group become aware of the world hunger problem. It could become an annual event.

Schedule your "Un-Dinner" and charge a fixed price—say, ten dollars per person. When your dinner guests arrive, however, they receive thirteen cents in change and the opportunity to purchase their "Un-Dinner" from a buffet table you have set up. Explain that each person's thirteen cents represents the daily food budget of most of the poorest segments of the third and fourth world populations. Display the following entrees on your buffet with signs indicating price values.

Water—1¢

Coffee—6¢ a cup

Sugar—2¢

Milk—2¢

Saltines—1¢ each

Olives—2¢ each

Orange slices—8¢ each

Hard-boiled eggs—6¢ each

Carrots—3¢ each

Sweet pickles—2¢ each

Follow the "meal" with a discussion of the problems of world hunger and one's own personal involvement, perhaps supplemented by a video presentation (several good ones are available through organizations like Compassion International and World Vision International). Donate the profits from your "Un-Dinner" to a reputable relief agency or local rescue mission.

WATERMELON FEST

Paper napkins, salt shakers, aluminum foil sheets and a truckload of donated watermelons makes a great summertime fundraiser. Keep the melons cool in a large container with bags of ice. Pick an event (Fourth of July, after an evening service, softball league playoffs) that ensures a crowd and your watermelon fest will be a crowd pleaser. Charge by the slice and have a donation box available as you solicit additional donations to support your project.

Here are some fun games you can also use at your fest. People can purchase the watermelons they need to participate in these games:

WATERMELON GRAB. Hide all the watermelons (similar to an Easter egg hunt) and then divide into two groups—the "grabbers" and the "taggers." The grabbers go out and try to locate and bring back a watermelon to "home base" without being tagged by the taggers. If they are tagged, they must put the watermelon down on the spot where they were tagged and "go to jail" for three minutes. Grabbers may only be tagged while carrying a watermelon. The goal is to see how many watermelons can be successfully brought into home base within a given time limit. Switch sides and play again.

WATERMELON SACK RACE. This is just like a regular sack race, only the contestants must carry a watermelon as they hop along with both feet in the sack.

WATERMELON BALANCE. Each team is given a watermelon and a tennis racket. Players must carry the watermelon on the head of the racket to a goal and back. Players may hold the racket any way they want, but they may not touch the watermelon with any part of the body.

SPEED EATING AND SEED SPITTING CONTEST. Cut the watermelons into wedges and place them on a table. Divide into teams of three to five persons each. Each team gets a cup. On a signal, teams start eating watermelon and spitting their seeds into the cup. The team that fills up its cup with seeds first is the winner.

SEED SPIT-OFF. See who can spit their seeds the farthest.

SEED RACE. Charge each participant for an equal size slice and race to see who can dig out the most seeds within the time limit.

WATERMELON CARVING. Participants carve creative designs with a knife into the watermelon rind.

CHAPTER SIX

AUCTION ACTION

AN AUCTION IS A POPULAR AND FUN METHOD OF RAISING MONEY. People enjoy getting a bargain, or at least trying to get one. Almost everything imaginable—goods and services—may be auctioned. Money is raised by selling donated items to the highest bidder. Find yourself an auctioneer and put that auction gavel to work.

If your group decides to auction off large, expensive items, engage the services of a professional auctioneer for best results and maximum profits.

ABSENTEE AUCTION

You can have an auction without all the formalities. Collect a number of items and services that are auctionable. Have one of your young people who is good with computer graphics create an "auction sheet"—a listing of the items and services available. You can duplicate it and hand it out to potential bidders. Number each of the items. Also, create an "absentee bid ticket" on which people can place their bids and give them to the person in charge. They can mail them in, or they may be present to bid. Now have your group go out, contact people, and auction the items and services you have collected.

First Church Youth Group
ABSENTEE BID TICKET

Our group is conducting an auction that you don't need to attend. All the money raised will go to support our summer work camp in the inner city. Every dollar you bid will go to help renovate a day-care center for children living below the poverty level. Please look over the list of items and services we are auctioning and make a bid. Fill in the blanks below with the item number, item title, bid amount, your name, address, and phone number.

ITEM	TITLE	AMOUNT

Name _____

Address _____

City/State/Zip _____

Phone (_____) _____

You may also make a donation to our summer work camp. All gifts are tax deductible.

☐ Yes, I would like to financially support the youth group summer work camp with a donation! I have enclosed a check for $ _____.

☐ Yes, I will pray for the youth group as they travel and work in the inner city.

AUCTION TICKETS

You can charge a small fee to those participating in the auction. Each bidder purchases a ticket with a detachable, numbered stub that also qualifies them for a door-prize drawing that can be given away at the end of the auction.

You can use the door-prize drawing as an incentive to encourage people to attend your auction. This is a way to increase the money you wish to raise and to publicize the event without much added work.

BRING A TOY/TAKE A TOY

This idea works great in conjunction with the Kids' Stuff (see pages 72–73) or Toy Box (see page 77) Auctions. The idea is simple and it makes a great add-on money-maker. Advertise that anyone bringing a toy may take a toy. Charge a small fee for this toy-swapping service.

CELEBRITY PARAPHERNALIA AUCTION

If you're willing to do some research and invest a few dollars in postage, you can make $1000 or more with this idea. Several months before your auction, comb through your music CDs and tapes for the addresses of artists' management, ministries or agencies. Also, phone your local radio stations to get addresses of many popular authors, speakers, and comedians. For the addresses of movie and TV stars, sports celebrities, and singers, spend an afternoon in a library looking through *Who's Who Among Celebrities*. Now you're ready to do some letter writing.

Round up your youth group and spend an evening writing letters, stuffing envelopes, and licking stamps. The letters should follow this general line: You are raising funds for your youth group and would appreciate donated, autographed items for an upcoming auction. After you send the letters, sit back and wait. Your work is done—until auction time, that is.

Within several weeks, you'll begin receiving mail—autographed albums, pictures, T-shirts, books, and cassettes. It's not unusual to realize a response rate of nearly fifty percent. Now it's auction time! Obtain the services of a humorous auctioneer and an assistant to display the donated items.

Then, let the fun begin. Hold an auction at your church or youth organization and sell the items to the highest bidders.

CHANCE AUCTION

Auction a few selected items off in this manner. Sell everyone tickets for a small fee. On the back of each ticket, bidders write their names, addresses, phone numbers and their bids and place them in a box next to the items they wish to win in the chance auction. When their item comes up for auction, the auctioneer randomly draws two tickets. The item goes to the highest bidder of these two tickets.

CRAZY AUCTION

Here is a good fundraiser for a large group. An article of value is put up for bid and the bidding starts at five cents. The person who bid the nickel tosses in his money immediately upon making his bid. The auctioneer announces that the five cent bid has been paid and then raises the bidding to ten cents. The one who bids ten cents tosses in his dime as a firm commitment of his intention. The auctioneer tries to raise the bidding and someone may bid a quarter, whereupon she tosses in the twenty-five cents, making the total in the pot forty cents. (Have plenty of change available to break large bills.) The bidding continues until no one bids again and then the article goes to the last person to bid. All of the previously paid money stays in the pot as well as the final bid. It is easy to sell a pair of shoes for two dollars when there are actually eleven dollars in the pot.

CREATE YOUR OWN AUCTION

Your group can organize creative auction packages. These can be stand-alone auctions, or packages to be auctioned off as part of a larger auction. Here are some sample ideas to get your creative juices flowing:

PARTY-IN-A-BOX. Package up things such as fast food coupons, free video rental coupons, tickets to sporting events, and passes to amusement parks.

THE KITCHEN SINK AUCTION. Put together for auction items with a kitchen/household theme such as microwave ovens, dishwasher, irons, hibachis, toasters, vacuum cleaners and the like.

SERVICES AUCTION. Auction services such as babysitting, financial planning, beauty makeovers, tax preparation, upholstery service, maid service, cleaning service, or pest control service.

MEMBERSHIP AUCTION. Auction memberships to athletic clubs, zoos, art museums, the symphony, etc.

THE GREAT GETAWAY AUCTION. Sell off vacation packages donated by airlines, travel agencies, and resorts.

THE GARAGE SALE AUCTION. Collect stuff that normally would be sold at a garage sale from your members, and auction as much of it as you can.

GOODIES AUCTION

This is a great activity that makes money off of someone else's planning. Talk with your adult leadership about auctioning off desserts at an adult social event. Your group does not organize the function but piggybacks on what is already planned. Your young people can bake or solicit donations of a number of delicious pies and cakes. The young people talk to the adult group about the project to which the money is going. Then, with slices of pie and cake in hand (on trays), your kids mingle with the adults seated at the tables, auctioning off the goodies to the highest bidders. Anyone purchasing a goody receives a free cup of coffee or tea. Practice with your young people before the auction begins so they are comfortable with raising the prices. The larger the group of adults, the more young people can be circulating with their goody trays. Keep the auctioneers moving for more fun and laughs and larger profits. Staple donation envelopes to the paper plates holding the goodies for those who wish to give an additional amount to your group's cause. You can then pass a basket or have a donation box at the exits to collect the donation envelopes.

INAUDIBLE AUCTION

This fundraiser will leave your group speechless. It works best in combination with another event like a dinner or musical program. You can even use this in combination with another fundraiser.

Like any auction, you will need to collect a variety of donated items that people would want to purchase. Place the items in a conspicuous place at your event with a sign announcing your intentions. Here's how it works.

Beside each of the items you are auctioning, place a sheet of lined paper. This is the bid sheet. At the top of each bid sheet, place the name of the item to be auctioned. Down the sheet, place the numbers one to ten. At the beginning of your event, explain to the group in attendance that if they like they can participate in an "inaudible auction." People can participate throughout the course of whatever event is taking place at the same time. All they need do to participate is write their name, phone number and bid amount on the bid sheet. Throughout the event, they can periodically check those items upon which they have placed bids. If another bid has been placed, they can write down a higher one on the line below the previous bid. At the close of the event, time is called and the bid sheets are collected. The items then go to the highest bidders—after they have paid your treasurer.

KIDS' STUFF AUCTION

Moms and dads are always looking for deals on kids' stuff. Here is an auction where they can get some great deals and give to your worthy cause. Your group can collect a boatload of items out of their own homes and the homes of friends and neighbors. Merchants may also donate items and services. You can then hold an auction (with plenty of baby-sitters to watch the kids!) while mom and dad spend the bucks. Here is a partial list of items that can be auctioned:

- baby furniture—changing tables, dressers, etc.
- baby accessories—strollers, high chairs, playpens, and walkers
- baby-sitting services from your group members
- toys and games
- school supplies—backpacks, notebooks, pencils and paper
- tutoring
- family pass to the zoo

- a birthday party at a fast food restaurant
- five free piano lessons
- playhouse
- children's books
- bikes
- training wheels
- children's cassette tapes
- clothing
- tuition to a sports or educational camp

MEAL OF FORTUNE

This fundraiser auction allows members of your church to participate as buyers, sellers, or both. Place a box in the church where people can leave a card with a brief description of a special meal they would be willing to prepare and serve in their home to the highest bidder. These meal plans may be anything from enticing specialty dishes to simple grilled hamburgers. Church members can submit as many meal plans as they like, specifying for each how many people the meal is for and whether it is for adults only or both adults and children.

Then, perhaps after a Sunday service, the meals can be auctioned off to the highest bidder without telling who will be preparing each one. After the auction, the buyer and seller agree on a convenient time when they could enjoy the meal together. All proceeds are collected at the time of the auction, and everything collected is profit. Best of all, this approach provides more opportunities for fellowship among church members.

MEGA-AUCTION

Get together with a number of other youth groups and plan a "Mega-Auction." You can combine your time, talents, resources and creativity to put together a very successful money-maker to support a single collective cause.

PANCAKE BREAKFAST/SERVANT AUCTION

This is a pancake breakfast with a twist. You begin Saturday morning with a traditional pancake breakfast. The young people wait tables and cook. Then a servant auction is held where the young people are auctioned off to do yard and house work at people's homes. Find someone who has fun being an auctioneer and who can creatively ensure that the young people are all auctioned off at about the same price (no hard feelings please). The adult youth workers clean up the breakfast mess after the auction while the young people work until noon at the home of whomever purchased their services.

PLAY-IT-AGAIN AUCTION

People are always searching for a deal on sports-related things. Thus, a play-it-again auction will appeal to them. Collect people's used sports equipment, solicit donations of new equipment and services like free golf lessons, tennis lessons, golf course green fees and the like from merchants. Here is a partial list of items and services for your group to consider:

- Backpacks
- Badminton sets
- Baseball caps
- Baseballs, bats, gloves
- Basketballs
- Boats
- Bowling balls
- Camping equipment
- Croquet sets
- Fishing rods
- Footballs
- Gift certificates to athletic shoe stores
- Gift certificates to sporting goods/ athletic stores
- Golf clubs, case of golf balls
- Hockey equipment
- Home video games
- Horseshoe sets
- Hot air balloon ride
- Hot tub
- Lacrosse equipment
- One-month memberships to athletic clubs or gyms
- Mountain bikes
- Pinball machines
- Pingpong table with pingpong set
- Pool tables
- Portable volleyball sets
- Raquetballs and racquets
- Skateboards
- Skates, rollerblades
- Skiing equipment
- Sleeping bags
- Sunglasses
- Surfboards
- Weekend ski trip
- Workout equipment

POTLUCK AUCTION

One great way to raise money for your group is to sponsor a potluck dinner and invite your entire church congregation, or only the parents and friends of your youth organization to attend. Those whose last names begin with the first half of the alphabet can bring a main dish, the other half a salad. Have your youth provide the dessert, coffee, and punch. They can also be responsible for serving and cleanup.

Ask each family to bring along a "gift" to be auctioned off—special cakes or pies, other baked goods, handcrafted items or household goods of some value. Place these items on a table and invite everyone to view them during the dinner hour.

After the tables have been cleared, auction off each item, saving the most expensive items for last. If there is someone in your church or youth organization with auctioneer experience, try to take advantage of that. Otherwise, find a person who can "ham it up" and generate lots of enthusiasm for every item.

SECRET BIDS

This is a simple technique that you can use for certain high-interest items. Have the bidders write down their bids, place them in an envelope you provide and hand them in. The item goes to the highest sealed bid.

SECRET BID SHEET

Bidder's Name _____

Phone (_____) _____

Item Number _____

Item Title _____

Bid Amount_____

TIME, TALENT, AND GOODS AUCTION

To raise funds you can auction off not only items but also special services provided by both youth and adults. Each young person should donate three or four items (such as garage-sale type items, homemade pies, or handcrafted gifts) and services (such as baby-sitting or yard work). Others in the congregation can volunteer to do the same. Your youth might even want to work together with the men's and women's groups in the church to make some items—the time they spend together will probably be as valuable as the auction itself.

In your publicity (which should begin six or eight weeks before the event), provide a list of items and services to be auctioned, along with the beginning bidding price for each. If possible, display some of the items in the church ahead of time so folks can see what they're bidding on.

The night of the auction, each person interested in bidding should register his or her name and receive an auction card with a number on it. The workers at the registration table should also keep track of who buys what. Have one or two adults act as auctioneers. You might also want to serve refreshments. At the end of the evening, buyers pay for their purchases at the registration table as they leave.

THE TOY BOX AUCTION

Ask people to donate toys their grown kids no longer use. These make great auction items since parents and kids alike are always looking for good deals. Those not auctioned off can be donated to charity. This is a good one to use with the Kids' Stuff Auction (see pages 72–73).

VINTAGE T-SHIRT AUCTION

There are probably piles of vintage T-shirts stuck away in closets all over your town. Don't use them as rags for the car wash or merely give them away, collect them and sell 'em!

Advertise the auction with the antiquity of the shirts ("T-shirts Dating Back as Far as 1972!") being the main focus. If you do not have especially old ones, confiscate an old college T-shirt from one of your adult volunteer workers and surprise the kids with it. Start the bidding and watch the fun as the young people buy replacements for their own T-shirt collections, shirts from events they never heard of, and shirts for their teddy bears.

YARD SALE AUCTION

This auction can be conducted as a stand-alone or as a supplement to an already existing auction you plan to hold. Ask for donated items that could be sold at a yard sale. Using various themes, put a variety of items together in a box. (Include items left over from your last yard sale.) Announce ahead of time that the items found in the boxes are those that would be found at a typical yard sale, flea market, or swap meet. Cover the boxes with newsprint so their contents cannot be seen. Give each of the boxes an interesting name that provides a clue to its contents. For example, you could auction off boxes with names like "The Green Thumb," "Family Fun," "The Toy Box," or "The Book Mark." Then auction away.

CHAPTER SEVEN

SPECIAL SERVICES

YOUR GROUP CAN RAISE MONEY INDIRECTLY FROM DONORS both inside and outside the church by providing services. Offering services for a flat fee, hourly rate or a donation requires that you have a number of willing and able volunteers who are ready to work. Your group can also create their own special services fundraisers by brainstorming all the unmet needs in your locale. Then put together your own special services.

AIRPLANE WASH

This is a great fundraiser for those kids in your group who love flying and airplanes. Contact your local airport about the possibility of having a "plane wash." Most airplane owners will usually pay plenty to have their planes washed (and waxed). All it requires is plenty of hoses, buckets, rags, towels, soap, and kids to do the work. And it only takes a few airplanes to make the effort financially worthwhile.

CAR WASH INCENTIVES

Car washes are a popular way to raise money for youth group projects. They are usually easy to organize, can be a lot of fun for young people, and most people need to have their cars washed. The best way to make the car wash as profitable as possible is to sell tickets in advance. All of the young people in the youth group receive a stack of car-wash tickets to sell during the weeks prior to the car wash date. Most people will buy a ticket even if they are unable to bring their car in for a wash.

FIRST CHURCH YOUTH

Interior & Exterior Car Wash

$3.00 donation
TO BENEFIT YOUTH CAMP

Saturday, February 2, 10 A.M.– 4 P.M.
Standard Station—Speedway at Channel Dr.

If your car wash is being used to help defray the costs of summer camp, or some other activity which requires that each kid come up with a certain amount of money, here's a good way to allocate the money fairly and provide incentive for the kids to sell tickets. With every ticket they sell in advance, they receive half the ticket price off their camp registration fee. For example, if a young person sells ten tickets at two dollars each, she or he receives ten dollars off the cost of camp. So the more tickets each young person sells, the less it costs him or her to go to camp.

On the day of the actual car wash, the young people who are washing cars have a chance to earn the other half of the ticket price. For every ticket that is redeemed, the young people washing cars at the time get the other half of the price, divided equally between them. On car wash tickets that are sold on location, 100% of the money goes to the young people for washing cars at that time. If a ticket is not redeemed, then half of that ticket price goes to overhead, transportation, and the like.

A system such as this insures that the young people themselves receive the benefit—proportional to the work they've put in. All money should be turned in to the youth leader or treasurer and allocated according to records that are kept. The kids need not handle the money themselves, or keep the money. All money that comes in reduces the cost of camp. Obviously, this system requires some record keeping and mathematics, but it's reasonable and fair.

DOGGIE DIP

For an unusual fundraiser that would work with any size youth group, try having a Doggie Dip. Advertise that your youth will wash dogs (pets) on a certain Saturday for a small fee. Most dog owners hate to wash their dogs, so the response will undoubtedly be tremendous.

Get together lots of metal or plastic tubs, some dog shampoo, towels, and hoses—and be ready for everything from bloodhounds to beagles! The owners should stand nearby to help calm the animals.

DOOR-TO-DOOR CAR WASH

Send your young people and adults out in groups of two or three armed with buckets, sponges, rags, soap, and squeegees. They go door-to-door and offer "house call" car washes. All the car owner needs to supply (in addition to the fee) is the water. The convenience of an in-your-own-driveway car wash usually yields generous donors.

GOLF CLUB WASH

Here's a unique fundraiser that gets good results. Set up a booth at the eighteenth green of a local golf course or in front of the clubhouse and offer to wash golf clubs for the tired hackers. All you need is permission from the golf course pro (or park board in the case of municipal courses), a pail of soapy water, a brush, a pail of clean water, a coin collector, and a few towels. For extra service, you may want to wax the woods and use a metal polish on the irons. If the money is going to a worthy cause, most golfers will be glad to pay a reasonable price.

If you set up in front of the clubhouse, give each golfer a ticket that identifies his or her golf bag, so they can go inside while you work, if they wish. You can also offer, for an additional fee, a waxing service where your group members will wax golf club covers and bags with saddle soap.

HIRE A SUPERKID

This is basically an "employment service" for your youth group. Most unemployed young people have lots of time on their hands after school and on weekends. You and your church can help them to find part-time jobs that give them meaningful work and also raise money.

To make it happen, print up an attractive flyer that includes information on all of the jobs that your kids can do: mow lawns, wash cars, baby-sit, clean house, paint, fix cars, care for pets, and so on. Distribute the flyers around town and wait for the calls to start coming in. Chances are the response will be very good. Assign the jobs that come in to your kids according to their abilities, and give them the responsibility to complete a quality job. If the customer is satisfied, chances are good that they will become a "regular customer." When the jobs start thinning out, send out more flyers and/or seek other free publicity, like the community notices in your local newspaper.

Employers can either pay the young people or pay the youth group. You might want to work out a system where a percentage of the money goes toward the youth group project, and the rest is kept by the young person to be used any way he or she wants.

INVENTORY CREW

Call large retail stores in your city and volunteer for "group inventory." Every store has to take a periodic inventory and usually needs temporary help to do it. They'll pay at least minimum wage, which can be a good fundraiser for the youth group.

PARENTS' NIGHT OUT

This is a good way to give the adults in your church a night out, provide a service project for your youth, and make a little money for your worthy cause. Offer the parents and/or adults a night out that gives them dinner, a movie, and babysitting all for one low price. Appropriate movies can be rented.

Have the entire group prepare and set up for the dinner. Then have one half serve the adults while the other half feeds and cares for the kids in another room. Then they switch. Half the group does cleanup, while the other half baby-sits. Afterward, all the youth work together to put everything away.

TASK-TRADIN' TICKET

Sell coupons like the ones pictured on page 84 for a fast and fun fundraiser. The tickets entitle buyers to an hour of work from the student seller. You may want to design two tickets—one with a higher purchase price for more strenuous work or more than one hour of work, and one with a lower price for easier work or just an hour of work. You can list on the tickets the types of work that can be done.

TASK TRADIN' TICKET

MINIMUM DONATION $2.00

This ticket entitles the bearer to one hour of work from the youth-group member whose signature is below:

Youth's signature _____

Youth's phone number _____

(See reverse side for work agreement)

THIS TICKET IS NOT TRANSFERABLE

All arrangements for the completion of the one hour of work will be made between the young person and the bearer of this ticket. No unreasonably strenuous work beyond the young person's capacity will be allowed. All proceeds from this ticket will be used for

Name of function _____

THIS TICKET MUST BE USED BEFORE

Date _____

FIRST CHURCH YOUTH GROUP

CHAPTER EIGHT

PLEDGE-A-THONS

PLEDGE-A-THONS ARE POPULAR FUNDRAISERS. Their popularity makes it easy to sign up sponsors who pledge money for every mile, hour, event or other measurement. You can net thousands of dollars with a well organized event. People generally are more willing to pledge when they know up front what their total commitment will be. Have your group members estimate the total pledge when they sign up their sponsors.

Most sponsors of Pledge-a-Thons do honor their pledge amounts. Some will even pay in advance (we suggest you encourage this). But you will need to teach the young people, possibly through role-play, the specifics of collecting a pledge. Let them practice on each other before they go out in the real world of pledge collection.

We have included a sample pledge sheet on page 91 so that you have an example from which to work. You will need to create a packet of information for each participant that includes a pledge sheet, a participant registration form, event rules, event specifics like the date, times, and information on where the pledged money will go, instructions on how to get sponsors, how to collect the pledged money, and what to do with the collected money. The larger the event, the more formal, professional and organized this packet will need to be. Groups sponsoring large Pledge-a-Thons that raise $10,000 to $50,000, print this packet in a brochure form that is attractive, easy to read and has all the necessary information clearly arranged.

ALUMINUM MAN TRIATHLON

You can create a spoof of the popular Ironman Triathlon (26.2 mile run, 2.5 mile swim, and 112 mile bike ride) competition by organizing an Aluminum Man Triathlon. All your group needs to do is put together a triathlon of gonzo sporting events. For example, play an hour of Wacky Volleyball (you make up wacky rules like the ball must bounce once before it is hit), two hours of the world's largest squirt gun fight, and tug-of-war in a giant mud puddle.

Collect pledges per hour of competition and whip your group into shape with a pre-event training table filled with pepperoni pizza.

LAWN-A-THON

This is a unique way to raise money for your group. Line up as many young people as you can and provide lawn mowers and transportation for each of them. Advertise with flyers and posters that on a certain Saturday, your group will mow lawns for free! Get as many people as you can to sign up to have their lawn mowed.

Now, for the money-making part. Pass out pledge sheets to all of your youth and have them get people to pledge twenty cents, fifty cents, or whatever for each lawn that your group mows from 6:00 A.M. to 6:00 P.M. that day. This not only raises money for your group, but also provides a real service for people in your community.

MEMORIZE-A-THON

Here's a fundraising "a-thon" that has spiritual benefits for your group as well as financial ones. Have a Bible Verse Memorize-a-Thon where your youth get pledges for every Bible verse that they learn. It's a contest that many people in your church will be eager to support.

You might want to establish some guidelines to avoid kids "learning" verses that are already well-known. Pick out certain portions of Scripture that everyone must memorize. Place a maximum limit on the number of verses. When it comes time for payment, all pledgers have the right to ask the kids to quote the verses they have learned.

READ-A-THON

This has also been called a "Bible-a-Thon," but the "Read-a-Thon" is a little more flexible. The idea is simply to choose a weekend or other period of time when the group continuously reads from the Bible or other Christian literature for as long as possible. One group we know of reads from the Bible nonstop from Friday afternoon until the Sunday morning service. One person would read while everyone else in the group sat in the audience and followed along. The readers would switch off, each reading for as long as he or she could. The group was able to read all of Genesis, Exodus, Joshua, Judges, Ruth, 1 Samuel, 2 Samuel, 1 Kings, 2 Kings, Job, Psalms, Proverbs, Ecclesiastes, Song of Solomon, Isaiah, Jonah, Daniel, Matthew, John, Acts, Romans, 1 and 2 Corinthians, Galatians, Ephesians, Philippians, 1 and 2 John and Revelation.

Each young person obtains sponsors for herself or himself. The sponsors pledge a certain amount for each hour of continuous reading. For example, thirty young people receiving about five dollars per hour in pledges can raise around $3,600 in one twenty-four-hour day. But what makes this fundraiser really different is that you can also arrange to have someone record the entire Read-a-Thon on cassette tapes. These tapes can then be used to provide either the Bible or other literature on tape to elderly people who find it difficult to read, or to the blind. When it is recorded, it also insures that the kids will read without messing up too much.

The advantage to reading something other than Scripture is that there is always the danger that kids might get so sick of reading the Bible after this ordeal that they will never pick it up again. You might consider reading C. S. Lewis, Madeline L'Engle, or any other good literature that kids can learn from as well as enjoy. But the Bible can be used so long as the experience is a good one, a lot of fun, and not forced upon anyone. Be sure to give kids periodic breaks (five to ten minutes per hour) to eat, stretch, go to the bathroom, and so on. Have the young people get plenty of rest before the event, and allow them to quit whenever they want to.

ROCK-A-THON

A twenty-four-hour "Rock-a-Thon" involves everyone in the group and serves as a great fundraiser. Each participant signs up sponsors at a certain amount for every hour he rocks in his rocking chair. Here are the rules:

1. Everyone provides his or her own rocking chair.

2. Each participant must rock at least four successive hours.

3. Time breaks are allowed only for trips to the bathroom.

4. The chair must be moving at all times.

Hold the event in a large room and supply some TV sets, record players, radios, coffee, cookies and lemonade. Encourage the young people to read positive literature (that you can provide) while they rock. You can also hold discussions on critical topics like social action, abortion, or evangelism. Keep the participants awake with cheering and lots of cold, wet towels. Meals can be provided by the church, families, or whatever. After participants finish rocking, they are given an official time certificate to show their sponsors. Keep a master record of all participants and their times to make sure all sponsors' monies are collected. Take a lot of pictures, and invite a local television news station to film the event. Every two or three hours announce to the kids the amount of money raised. It keeps enthusiasm high.

SERVICE ROCK-A-THON

A new dimension is added to the Rock-a-Thon idea when the youth pledge an hour of service for every hour they rock. For example, if twenty youth rock for twelve hours, the entire group pledges 240 hours of service. The group can then work off the time by visiting shut-ins, going on service retreats and work camps, doing yard work for the disabled, and so on. Of course, you still get adult sponsors to give a certain amount of money per hour rocked, but the adults are much more willing to pledge if they know the youth are going to give something themselves by working.

STARVE-A-THON

This is an unusual program in which the youth meet together and go without food for twelve to twenty-four hours. (Of course, they are allowed water.) There are three main benefits to a program such as this:

1. Kids get a better understanding, in a small way, of what it means to be hungry.
2. People can "sponsor" the youth by paying them so much an hour for the period. The money can then be used to buy food for a poor family within the community, or to support a local food bank or other relief organization.
3. Your time together can be used to study the problems of poverty and hunger, and pray for those who struggle with chronic hunger.

Before beginning you can read up on the spiritual discipline of fasting in *The Spirit of the Disciplines* (Dallas Willard, Harper San Francisco, 1988) and *Celebration of Discipline* (Richard Foster, Harper & Row, 1978).

WORK-A-THON

The idea is to arrange jobs for the young people in elderly people's homes. The jobs could include painting, gardening, housekeeping, shopping, or any other service that the kids could perform. Top priority should go to elderly people from the church or community who cannot afford to pay for the work they need done. The young people then get donors to sponsor them for their work. On the arranged day, the young people work an eight-hour day at the different homes, free of charge to the people they are working for. Afterwards, they collect the amounts pledged by their sponsors. Set a due date for collections; this will make it easier for the young people to collect from their sponsors. One group made over $250 with only ten kids working. One girl in that group made $60 for eight hours work.

SAMPLE PLEDGE SHEET

We have provided a sample pledge sheet that you can adapt to your particular Pledge-a-Thon activity. We recommend that you let people know when they sign up how much their total pledge will be. People are more willing to give when they know up front how much they are being asked to donate.

The sample provided here has space for two pledgers. We recommend your form have ten to twelve spaces. You can provide additional pledge sheets to those kids who can obtain more than ten or twelve sponsors.

SPONSOR PLEDGE SHEET

MY GOAL IS TO RAISE $ _____

Name _____

Address _____

City/State/Zip_____

Phone (_____) _____

MAKE CHECKS PAYABLE TO FIRST CHURCH YOUTH GROUP

Sponsor #1

Name _____

Address _____

City/State/Zip_____

Phone (_____) _____

Pledge Amount _____
Total Pledge Amount: ☐ $10   ☐ $15   ☐ $20   ☐ $25
                      ☐ $35   ☐ $50   ☐ $75   ☐ $100   ☐ Other $ _____

☐ Pledge Pre-paid   ☐ Remind Me of My Pledge

Sponsor #2

Name _____

Address _____

City/State/Zip_____

Phone (_____)_____

CHAPTER NINE

ECO-CASH

YOUR GROUP CAN MAKE THE GREEN STUFF BY THINKING GREEN. Ecologically-minded groups can help heal God's earth (Rom. 8:18–25) and make money too! Here are only a few of the many possibilities your group should consider.

BUSINESS ECO-BUCKS

Area businesses can help your group raise money by donating their aluminum cans, glass and plastic bottles, and other recyclables. Create an attractive recycling box with your group's name and cause. Meet with store managers and business owners to sell your project. Create a strategy for regularly collecting the materials and delivering them to the appropriate recycling centers.

CANNED CASH

Recycling aluminum cans is good for God's earth and good for your group. All you need is a secure place to keep the cans, a means to transport them to a recycling center that pays you cash, and a great cause to motivate your group to collect them. Get the word out to the friends and supporters of your group that you are collecting the cans (and why!), provide a convenient place for the cans to be deposited, or collect them, and your project is off and running. You will need a secure place to store your stash to deter thefts.

The amount of money to be made recycling cans depends on the market. An average trailer load can weigh 150 pounds. At sixty cents a pound, a trailer load can net your group ninety dollars. An organized group can fill a trailer quickly, which means thousands can be made every year. This idea can easily be adapted if your area also offers cash for glass and plastic bottles.

CAN you help support youth missions?
Sure you CAN!

Bring your aluminum cans to the receptacles on the west side of the youth building. We will turn those cans into dollars to support our winter mission trip.

Thanks for your support.

TRASH into CASH!

Help turn trash into cash by picking up discarded aluminum cans. Bring these cans to the bin behind the youth building. Money collected will be used to fund summer youth camp scholarships.

Help us pick up cash by picking up cans.

COLOSSAL CLEANUP

Here's a profitable and dependable fundraiser that can become an annual project for your youth group. Contract with the management of your local fairgrounds or stadium, to do cleanup after a major event. The job usually takes about a day or so (depending upon the size of your group and the event) and can earn your group hundreds of dollars. With good organization and teamwork, this kind of job doesn't have to be overwhelming, and good work will pay off in getting next year's contract.

ECOLOGY WALK

This takes in two ideas and can be very successful if you have a group of over twenty-five people. First of all, as in a regular Walk-a-Thon, young people get sponsors. Then, as the young people walk, they pick up all the cans and bottles which litter the highways. Divide the young people into groups of five or six and send them in different directions with plastic bags. As they fill the bags, they leave them at the side of the road. Have someone follow along in a truck to pick up the full bags. If you have a good day, you can easily pick up between 500 and 1,000 pounds of cans and bottles which can be recycled for cash.

METAL MONEY MAKER

Turn metal that normally would make its way to the county dump into cash. Your group can collect all kinds of scrap metal—sheet metal, aluminum door frames, radiators, aluminum chairs, batteries, aluminum car bumpers, copper tubing and wire, iron, rain gutters, and hot water heaters. Call your local scrap metal yard to see what they are buying, then design a "Metal Money Maker" project with your group.

ECO-MUG A HOUSE
The flyer says it all.

GET YOUR HOUSE

ECO-MUGGED

The Senior Youth Group, in keeping with its environmental concern, wants to help you . . .

Help Us Save the Earth

How? By letting us "Eco-Mug" your house. We will come in at a pre-determined time and . . .

- Get your name off junk-mail lists
- Install a toilet dam
- Check the air in your tires for proper inflation
- Leave a hand-made Youth Group "Draft Dodger" to keep cold air from getting in under your door

- Install one faucet aerator
- Leave a hand-painted Youth Group Eco-Mug
- Leave you with three beautiful note cards printed on recycled paper
- Take your unwanted clothing to an appropriate donation center

What better gift to give to a friend and our world!
Cost for getting Eco-Mugged is $30.
All proceeds will go to our Youth Group Spring Break "Give 'Em a Break"

We estimate that if 100 families get Eco-Mugged we could each year . . .

SAVE
- 150 trees to sit under in the shade
- 622,000 gallons of fresh water to drink or swim in
- 3,000 gallons of gas which makes for cleaner air to enjoy
- 36,500 disposable cups from filling our dumps

HAVE
- 100 more comfortable houses to wait out winter's cold in
- 300 more people told about saving God's earth through letters written
- 100 more people living with better clothes and dignity*

*based on research done in *50 Simple Things You Can Do to Save the Earth*

☐ **YES!** I want my house **Eco-Mugged.** Here is my $30 gift to help save the earth.

Name _____

Address _____

_____

Phone (home) _____

(work) _____

PAPER BOOSTERS CLUB

In most areas it is possible to pick up some money by recycling used newspapers. It takes a lot of paper to make it profitable, but if organized properly, it can be a good way to raise dollars for your ongoing projects. Enlist members of your group and congregation as well as your neighbors to become members of the Paper Boosters Club. When they join (you can give them an official membership certificate), they promise to save all their newspapers for your group. Once a month, set up a paper collection route so that young people are sure to go around and pick up all the paper. If you get enough people involved, and stay with it over a period of time, you can earn a lot of money in this way.

RECYCLE-A-THON

Your group can pick a week or two during which to hold this "trash into cash" event. Call your local recycling business or businesses to see what the going rate is for various recyclable items from aluminum cans to newspapers to scrap metal. Create a list of all the things your group thinks they can recycle. Each group member then creates a list of individuals and businesses with whom they are familiar. Group members contact these people, telling them that on your designated day, the group will be conducting their Recycle-a-Thon. (You can give people more than a week's notice depending upon how organized an effort you choose to commit yourself to.) On the appointed day, the recyclable materials are collected.

TRASH-A-THON

One problem with most "a-thons" is that they accomplish little or nothing in themselves except raising money. The Trash-a-Thon, however, strikes a blow for a better environment as it makes the bucks. Young people, instead of sitting in a rocking chair, taking a hike or riding a bike, pick up litter.

They get people to contribute a set amount of money for each large trash bag full of litter they pick up. Select a good trashy spot for your Trash-a-Thon. Your city or county health department may be able to help you find the worst spot, which in this case is the best. (Make sure it is safe.) If the spot is good and cruddy, each kid can pick up fifteen to twenty bags in about five hours with no sweat. This project has appeal to the sponsors/donors in that they are helping to clean up their town as well as helping your kids. You may be able to talk local merchants into providing prizes for your young people as incentives, such as a prize for the person with the most sponsors, and another for the young person who picks up the most trash.

CHAPTER TEN

HOLIDAY FUNDRAISING IDEAS

HOLIDAYS, ESPECIALLY THANKSGIVING AND CHRISTMAS, often put people in a giving mood. Your group can design fundraisers to profit from this spirit of giving. With many of these ideas you will be able to help fund social action projects, because people are more than willing to give to help others during the holidays.

CHRISTMAS CRAFTS SALE IN SEPTEMBER

Selling Christmas crafts after Thanksgiving is not a novel idea. But holding this sale in September is! Publicize your event early, promoting a "beat the Christmas rush" theme. Pick up some artificial Christmas trees on the day of the sale and sell, sell, sell. You can solicit holiday gift certificates from local restaurants (to be used during the holidays) as door prizes.

CHRISTMAS GIFTS AUCTION

This December event is part publicity and part fundraiser but you'll have to start a couple months earlier to pull it off. If you do, it may become a tradition with your group. The idea is simple:

First, determine how the money you'll raise from the auction will be used. Second, solicit new merchandise from area businesses—items like lift tickets to ski areas, gift certificates to restaurants, autographed basketballs (solicit these from professional sports teams in your area), quilts, dolls—anything! Assign one young person to a business so they aren't bombarded by multiple requests for merchandise. Carefully draft a letter for your young people to use when introducing themselves, and explaining the auction's purpose. In addition to mentioning the tax deduction available on these donations, sweeten the deal further by offering to run free ads in the auction program that you will distribute not only to all auction goers, but also to your church congregation or organization membership.

Third, a week before the auction, send an announcement or a press release about the auction to your local radio stations and newspapers. Any coverage they give is free publicity. Finally, have your auction! Be sure to have one or two good auctioneers who can keep things moving for an afternoon.

An early December date for the auction is ideal for many who want to get a large share of their Christmas shopping done before the last-minute rush!

CHRISTMAS MISSIONARY DINNER

For this special Christmas activity, have your church youth group select some missionaries living abroad that the church supports. The group should get to know the missionaries they have chosen by corresponding with them. Then begin making plans for a Christmas Missionary Dinner some time in November. Hang Christmas decorations and post pictures or letters from the missionaries so that people can see them. The youth group can cook and serve the meal, which could include some dishes from the country where the missionaries are serving. Adults of the church are invited to the dinner, and following a talent show by the youth and a presentation of the work being done by the missionaries, the people are asked to give a free-will offering. The offering can then be sent to the missionaries as a "Christmas bonus," which they ordinarily would not get. It is a good idea to hold this event as early as possible as it takes a long time to send money overseas.

CHRISTMAS POST OFFICE

Here's a Christmas season fundraising activity. Set up a "Christmas Post Office" to beat inflation and slow mail service. It can be fancy (construct a box out of plywood, with little compartments large enough for letters and Christmas cards) or it can be just a table. Place it in a prominent place in your church, announcing that "The Christmas Post Office is now open."

The church members drop off Christmas cards intended for others in the church. They pay either what they would normally pay in postage, or just give a donation to the "postmaster." The young people sort the mail and give it out to the appropriate people at the end of the service. For a good service project, the young people can also deliver cards to shut-ins and those that didn't come by. You might also begin a "singing telegram" service for a set fee. Once you begin this service, the church members will be looking for it every Christmas. More people send cards when they know the money is going toward a good cause. One church has done this for three years in a row and each year it's more successful than the last.

CHRISTMAS SITTER SERVICE

As a fundraiser and service project at Christmas, members of your youth group, with adult supervision, can staff the church's nursery several evenings the first two weeks of December. For a fee or donation, parents of children up to age ten can then drop off their kids between 6:00 and 10:00 P.M. while they go Christmas shopping. Most adults really appreciate this kind of service.

CHRISTMAS TREE OF LOVE

At Christmas time, put a Christmas tree (either real or artificial) in the church foyer. Place a few decorations on the tree, but leave it embarrassingly bare. Leave a package of ornament hangers under the tree, along with a donation box, decorated to look like a gift. Ask people to consider hanging one of their Christmas cards on the tree with greetings to the entire congregation as an alternative to sending out individual cards to everyone. The card can be hung on the tree by using one of the ornament hangers provided.

Ask the people to donate the money they save in cards and postage to your project. The money can be deposited in the gift box under the tree. People can give more than the money they save if they choose. People are generally more responsive to this if you have a specific project in mind, such as a missionary project, providing toys or other gifts for an orphanage, or giving to a hunger relief agency. Be sure to stress that this project is optional. If people still wish to send personal greeting cards, they should be encouraged to do so.

CHRISTMAS TREE PICK-UP SERVICE

Here's a simple fundraiser for your youth group. Spend one or two days after Christmas (before school starts up again) going around with trucks picking up discarded Christmas trees, oversized gift boxes, and the like. Advertise the pick-up service in advance, both in the church and throughout the area. You can even have it announced in the local newspapers and on radio stations. Have people donate the use of trucks, and your only expense will be gas and the fee, if any, to dump the trees at your local dump. Charge a flat fee for the service, or you can accept donations. This is an especially good idea because many refuse disposal companies will not pick up Christmas trees, or they charge extra for it.

DELIGHTFUL DESSERTS

As the holiday season approaches, your group can raise funds by advertising "Delightful Desserts" for sale. Simply distribute a list of baked goodies which your youth, their parents, and others in your group or congregation would be willing to bake and donate. Then take orders. This way you know ahead of time exactly how many items you'll sell, and you'll avoid the confusion of baking too many or too few goodies. Since the baked goods are donated, the receipts are pure profit.

GIFTS FOR JESUS

This year, why not invite your kids to do a Christmas gift exchange in which they actually purchase gifts and give them to Jesus? Set a price limit on the gifts, or have the young people make them by hand. They should be wrapped like any Christmas gift would be, and placed in a manger at the party or meeting. Allow each young person to open her or his gift (break into small groups if your group is large), explain why it was chosen, and tell how Christ can use it. For example, someone might give a pair of new shoes, and tell about an orphanage which needs new shoes for its children.

By giving to "one of the least of these" (Matt. 25:31–40), the gift is actually given to Christ. This can be a meaningful way for young people to understand the true spirit of Christmas, and a way for you to collect items for a service project without having to raise the money to pay for them.

GIFT-WRAPPING FUNDRAISER

Once your young people begin their Christmas vacation, but before Christmas, plan a fundraising gift-wrap service at a local discount store. Buy your wrap, boxes, and ribbon from a paper company at wholesale prices; and a few nights before the fundraiser, rent a bow machine and make your bows. Set up shop in the store's layaway department and ask the manager to announce your service over the public address system throughout the day. Last-minute shoppers are usually in a panic and extremely grateful for your services.

This fundraiser can also be set up in your church. Kids could wrap gifts before and after services and social functions during the month of December. With a little advance publicity, this can be a real winner!

HALLOWEEN FUN HOUSE

Groups around the country have earned thousands of dollars with this idea. There are organizations that fund most of their projects with this one. Halloween Fun Houses require a lot of work, time and publicity, but the payoff is usually big. If no one else in your town is doing one, a fun house may be for your group. We recommend that if your group chooses this as a fundraiser, emphasize the scary and avoid occult/satanic and bodily violence/mutilation themes. A fun house can be lots of fun and there are a number of scary special effects and practical jokes that are in good taste (see *Ideas Combo* Issue Number 21–24 published by Youth Specialties).

HOLIDAY ART

Put your artistic young people to work decorating the windows of area businesses for the holidays with tempera paints. Your outgoing young people can sell the idea to merchants, fast food establishments and other local businesses for a flat fee. When the business people are presented with your worthy cause, they are usually more than willing to pay for your services.

HOLIDAY-GRAMS

Everyone likes to get surprises at holiday times. A Holiday-Gram is a greeting attached to a candy treat which can be made, sold and delivered by your youth group.

You will need lots of yarn or ribbon and several yards of netting. These items can be purchased in holiday colors at any fabric store. You'll also need individually wrapped candy, and construction paper in colors related to the particular holiday (pastels for Easter, red and green for Christmas, etc.).

Schedule a "gram get-together." Decide on the shape for the card. Holiday cookie cutters make great patterns for this. Cards should be at least three inches square to allow room for the message. Cut out and punch a hole at the top of each one. Cut net into five-inch squares and place three to five pieces of candy inside. Gather edges of net together and tie with ribbon or yarn. Thread the ribbon or yarn through the hole in the card and tie into a bow. This is your Holiday-Gram. Place these in a box(es) and set them on a table in a high traffic area of your church. Advertise the date, time and location of your Holiday-Gram sale. Purchasers of the Holiday-Grams write a message on one side of the card and the person's name to whom it will be delivered on the other side. Purchased "Holiday-Grams" are delivered by your group members.

MEGA MERRY CHRISTMAS CARD

The residents of convalescent homes appreciate this gargantuan holiday greeting, although anyone will get a kick out of it. Lead your young people in cutting, taping, and papering or painting a refrigerator box so it resembles a huge Christmas card. You can write the greeting either to Jesus or to the residents themselves. What the residents like, of course, is to see their names on the card, so get a list of their names.

This becomes a fundraiser because you charge members of your church one dollar to sign the card. When you explain the purpose of the card and the project to which the donated dollar is going, most people are more than happy to sign, and you can collect signatures and dollars quickly. If your church is large, you may want to create cards for several convalescent homes.

A day or two before Christmas, take each card along as your group carols through the halls of each convalescent home. Take the mega-card into the rooms as you visit, pointing out the residents' names to them. Then leave the card in the cafeteria or living room area.

SINGING VALENTINE

Here is a good fundraiser that works best on Valentine's Day. The youth group simply invites members of the congregation to purchase a valentine for their sweethearts (secretly) on the Sunday before Valentine's Day. You can charge somewhere around five dollars per valentine. Then, on Valentine's Day, the youth group arrives at each sweetheart's house and delivers the surprise singing valentine. Your group members should all be dressed in red and several members can be dressed as Cupid. After singing romantic or silly love songs, present the sweetheart with a Certificate of Affection with the secret admirer's name on it. Don't limit this activity to valentines. Deliver flowers or candy for an extra fee. The elderly and shut-ins especially appreciate receiving a surprise singing valentine.

THIRTY PIECES OF SILVER

At Easter time, an effective way to receive a special offering from your youth for a worthwhile project is to have everyone bring a plastic sandwich bag with thirty pieces of silver in it (the amount for which Jesus was betrayed). Any denomination of coin is acceptable, so long as it is silver. You can then discuss the betrayal and death of our Lord and how all of us have betrayed Christ through our sin, hence the reason for his death and resurrection.

VALENTINE BALLOONS

Your group can make money on Valentine's Day by selling and delivering helium balloons. Have the kids take orders three weeks prior to the holiday. Then make arrangements with a local balloon or stationery store to supply you with balloons and helium at wholesale prices (or maybe even at cost). Each person ordering a balloon should fill out an order card with the name, address, and phone number of the balloon recipient, and the seller's name. Leave a space on the other side of the card for a message from the sender to the recipient. The customer then pays for the balloon and returns the card to the seller. Collect all the cards several days before Valentine's Day and group them by geographic areas.

On Valentine's Day, have two people come early to fill the balloons and attach the messages. The rest of the group can show up about an hour later to deliver them. It's simple, and you can also use this idea for other holidays.

CHAPTER ELEVEN

SPECIAL EVENTS

PUT THE FUN BACK INTO FUNDRAISING by sponsoring a party or other social event. Any social or special event can be turned into a fundraiser with a concession stand as well as ticket sales. And making money through social events is often supported by churches who frown on traditional fundraisers.

BIGGER AND BETTER HUNT

This idea can be used at a social event for a great time and to raise money as well. The entire group meets at a central location for instructions. The group is divided into small groups of four or five. Each team is given a penny to begin with, and they are then dispersed to knock on doors in a given neighborhood. Their goal: to trade the penny for something bigger and better. They then take the item they received in trade for the penny to the next house and again attempt to trade that item for something bigger and better. They are not allowed to trade for cash; it must be an item that the person at each house is willing to give in exchange for whatever the team has at the time. Team members are not allowed to "sweeten the pot" by adding more money to the original penny or altering any of the items along the way.

Each team has one hour. At the end of the time limit, the teams meet back at the central location and display what they finally ended up with. The group with the biggest and the best item is the winner. This has been used successfully with many different groups, and some groups have traded for such items as washing machines, watermelons, electric toasters—all kinds of very usable stuff. The items collected can be sold in a rummage sale or auction, and the money raised can then be used for your cause.

BIGGER AND BETTER HUNT (REVISED)

Here's a fundraising version of the Bigger and Better Hunt. Divide your group into teams and give each team several pennies. Set a time limit, tell the teams what prize the winners will get, then start the event. Each team goes door-to-door throughout the neighborhood, informing residents that they are members of the youth group and are raising money for whatever cause. Then they say. "May I trade you this penny for any money amount that is bigger and better?" Teams will probably receive a nickel, dime, or quarter for the penny, which at the next house they attempt to trade up. This continues until the original penny becomes a dollar. Then teams start over with a penny again. It's surprising how much you can make in only an hour. And there are other advantages: no complicated planning is required for this fundraiser, your teenagers see money coming in immediately, large donations are not required, and it's an excellent opportunity to establish a name for yourselves in the community. A great time will be had by all!

CHRISTIAN DINNER THEATER

Here's an idea that is not only an excellent fundraiser, but helps build community with youth and adults. The Christian Dinner Theater begins with a gourmet meal, served by appropriately costumed youth waiters and waitresses in a gaily decorated room. The tables should be adorned with fresh flowers and candles. Dinner music is provided by the youth to add to the theater atmosphere. After dinner, provide a musical interlude utilizing talent of all ages. Then the youth present a play or sketch. Afterwards, you can have refreshments, a dance, or an after-theater party where your kids can mingle with the audience.

In order for this activity to generate a good amount of funds for your project, it is important to (1) get as much of the food and decorations donated as possible, (2) promote it well, and (3) ask for donations above and beyond the cost of the meal tickets. Be sure to ask for donations during the weeks of preparation for the dinner and play, not just on the evening of the play. One group of fifty young people who participated in this activity raised close to $4,000 from gifts, donations and tickets. Good luck!

DRIVE-IN MOVIE NIGHT

If your church has a big parking lot, or if you have another large area that's usable, here's a great event that can be used as a fundraiser, or just for fun. Use four large sheets on a building as a screen. You will also need a sixteen millimeter projector, a few large speakers, and a movie to show. You can then have a drive-in movie in your church parking lot and invite all of your church and neighborhood to come. Charge admission per car or per person.

If you are in a heavily populated neighborhood, check with local authorities and with the neighbors about the noise that will be generated. If that is a problem, find a more suitable area.

You can also set up a refreshment stand and sell soft drinks, popcorn, hot dogs and candy. Make sure you show the movie on a warm night, and encourage people to bring chairs, chaise lounges, and so on. Be sure and book a good film that everyone would want to see, as well as a couple of shorts (like cartoons) and advertise the event well. You might even put an ad in the theater section of your local newspaper. With plenty of advance planning and enthusiasm, an event like this can be a real success.

55+ PARTY

This intergenerational social will provide a fun way for your group to raise money for missions and interact with senior adults at the same time.

With the assistance of sponsors or parents, have the young people plan a special event for senior adults fifty-five and older. Be sure to include some senior adults in these planning sessions. Costs can be kept to a minimum by having the parents of your group members provide the food.

Each person fifty-five years and older pays ten cents per year of their age to attend the social. That means a sixty-eight-year-old attending the pot luck social pays $6.80.

Before the meal, members of your group can make a presentation explaining how the money will be spent. After the presentation, it's time to eat. The menu can be simple. You may want to have it reflect the culture of your mission field. Consideration should be made on the types of food to be served to the seniors. It is best to avoid food that is too spicy or difficult to chew. And remember those low-salt, low cholesterol diets.

The easiest way to serve the food is buffet-style Place all the food and serving items on a large table. For speedier service, allow people to pass on both sides of the table. Beverages such as coffee and punch can be served from a separate table.

To promote the intergenerational aspect of this social, assign group members to each table of senior adults. And after the meal, provide entertainment such as group singing and games. Special presentations by talented group members can add to the festive mood.

Follow up your dinner with a personal thank-you note to each senior adult who participated. Include a brief description of how the donor's money aided in your mission.

LE GRANDE CHATEAU

This fundraiser is great fun for everyone. The idea is to open for one night only your own fine French restaurant for an elegant dining experience that includes "classy" entertainment. The whole thing, however, is done slightly tongue-in-cheek. The catch is the small print at the bottom of the menu which reads: "Management reserves the right to make substitutions without patron consent!" So, regardless of what people order, they all get the same thing.

The menu should be elaborate and include extravagant dishes at high prices. It should look like a regular menu (with the exception of the catch line at the bottom, of

Le Grande Chateau

— Entrées —

Includes dinner roll, dessert, and hot beverage.

Storione á la Cardinale
$14.55

Bigginaccé de Ronaldois
$11.90

New York Steak
$12.20

Fischer Fried Chicken
$10.75

Veal Marengo and Gamberi
$18.60

Arthur's Perogy Geschmäck
$11.00

Dumpling Dewar Stew
$8.75

Lobster Waikiki
$20.65

Children's portions available upon request.

— Appetizers —

$6.00 each

Escargot   Galettes au Fromagé   Canapes

Frogs' Legs   Bongo Bongo

Floor Shows commence at 7:30 & 9:30 p.m.

Management reserves the right to make
substitutions without patron consent!

course). The publicity should include a snooty "reservations only" system so the right amount of food can be prepared. You can also have a dress code (ties for the gentlemen, please). Decorations should be as elegant as possible, with cut flowers, candles, and linen on the tables, and classical music playing in the background. The waiters should be dressed to the hilt, with the maitre'd in tux if possible. The food should be nice but simple. Juice, tossed salad, baked chicken, baked potato, vegetable, roll, and dessert. The program after the meal can be anything you want. Be sure to allow a few minutes to explain your project and how the proceeds of the evening will be used.

At the close, the waiters can present the "cheque" to each customer, instructing the diners to make their donations in any amount and to either pay their waiter or pay on their way out. Usually a special event like this gets very good results. It's worth all the work involved.

NON-ROCK FOR MISSIONS

If your group enjoys putting on musicals and special events, why not put together a creative package that caters to the interest of older people (who also have the bucks)? Ask some older (forty-five and up) individuals to help you identify and plan a musical concert for the older generation. You can often find talented musicians and orchestras in your area who will perform for a modest fee, or even donate their services. Sell tickets before the event and at the door and ask for a donation during a mid-concert break. You will be pleasantly surprised at the good response you can receive to support a worthy cause. One group raised over $20,000 with a well-planned event.

OLD-FASHIONED CARNIVAL FUN

Carnivals provide a fun event and make money for your organization as well. The work required by carnivals, however, does not always justify the money raised. But if you are looking for a social event first and a money-maker second, then a carnival may be just what your group wants.

Carnivals are the most fun and draw bigger crowds when you design them around a theme. For example, some churches use carnivals as an alternative to Halloween. One church sponsors an all day harvest holiday fair on the Saturday closest to Halloween. The key to a successful carnival is organization. You will need several committees (ticket sales, booth coordination and set-up, prize purchasing, coordination and distribution, food, publicity, etc.).

You will also need seed money to purchase the prizes, print tickets and publicize the event. And you will need plenty of volunteers to organize and work the carnival. Schools, and churches with schools, can do the best with carnivals. A large church or school can have the different ministries or classrooms take responsibility for different booths.

The most money is made when you sell advance tickets for a discounted price. For example, if you are selling tickets at your carnival at four for a dollar, you can sell advance tickets at five for a dollar.

Prizes can be purchased from a local carnival supply store or ordered through the mail (usually cheaper). Divide the prizes into categories depending upon their cost and desirability. Consolation prizes may be given to all preschoolers. You can get free catalogs from the following carnival supply companies:

Oriental Trading Company, Inc.
P. O. Box 3407
Omaha, NE 68103
(800) 228-2269

US Toy CO.
1227 East 119 Street
Grandview, MO 64030
(800) 255-6124

Age-graded booths will attract young and old alike. Try to create a variety of booths that appeal to the very young, to school-age children, to pre-teens, and to adults. Fifteen to twenty-five booths make for a good-sized carnival that can provide a variety of activities.

The number of tickets you charge will vary per activity. An air mattress jumping booth will require more tickets than a cake walk. The more sophisticated the activity, the more tickets you can charge.

Here are a few ideas to get your group's creative juices flowing. Ideas for booths are only limited by your group's imagination.

AIR MATTRESS JUMPING BOOTH *(Preschool through sixth grade)*. Rent one of those mega air mattresses that kids can jump around on from a carnival supply center. This activity will remain busy the whole time and keep kids at your carnival event.

CARTOONS IN A BUS *(Preschool)*. Set up a projector and screen or TV and VCR at the front of a school or church bus. Children enter from the rear and watch five to ten minutes of cartoons.

DECORATE A COOKIE *(All ages)*. This is always a popular activity for young children. Ask for donations of sugar cookies in different shapes and sizes as well as the sprinkles, frostings, raisins and spreads that make them delicious. Let kids choose three decorations from your assortment that they can use to decorate the cookie of their choice. Keep the decorating area clean and sanitary. Use separate plastic spoons and knives for each container of decoration.

DUCK POND *(Preschool to kindergarten)*. Small plastic ducks float in a "pond" which can be a cat litter box or similar container. The ducks are numbered on their bottoms #1, #2, and no number. Those players fishing out a duck (see Fish Pond) with #1 get the best prize, those with #2 are given a lesser prize and no numbers receive a handshake.

DUNKING BOOTH *(Anyone who can toss the ball)*. Get a dunking booth from a carnival supply store and ask local celebrities (you define) to be the dunkees. Frequently change dunkees.

ENTERTAINMENT *(all ages)*. This is not a booth but scheduled free shows that can feature puppets, choirs, juggling, musical instruments, skits, and clowning. Scheduled throughout the day with posted and publicized times, entertainment can attract large crowds and keep people at your carnival.

FISH POND *(Preschool to second grade)*. Poles with clothespins on the end of the line make fishing over a cubicle easy for this age group. A prize is secretly attached on the other side of the cubicle.

FOOD BOOTHS *(All ages)*. Much of the food can be donated, especially if you are a school. Ask the food distributors from whom your cafeteria purchases their food to donate items for your food booths. You could have a pretzel stand, lemonade stand, popcorn stand, cotton candy stand, hot dogs and soda booth, snow cone stand and much more.

HELIUM BALLOON SALES *(All ages)*. A walker carrying around helium-filled balloons for sale is always a big hit.

RING TOSS ON CANES *(Preschool to primary)*. Toss rings onto canes. The game can be purchased through US Toy CO. (800) 255-6124. Preschoolers have a six-foot throw; primaries have a nine-foot throw.

SAWDUST HUNT *(Six and under)*. Kids hunt through a box full of sawdust with their hands until they find a prize.

SOLAR SYSTEM BEAN BAG TOSS *(Preschool to third grade)*. A bean bag is thrown at planet targets (cardboard circles, painted to look like the planets and sized accordingly, hung on string and attached, in proper order, to a crossbar). A player gets three bags to throw. Any one bag that hits a large planet wins a small prize, with larger prizes awarded for smaller planets. Preschool: a six-foot throw gets a prize; primaries: a nine-foot throw with one or more hits gets a prize.

SUCKER GAME *(Preschool through sixth grade).* Players pick a sucker from a peg board and check the tip to see if there is a color for an additional prize along with the sucker. A plain tip is sucker only; a red tip wins a prize.

TENNIS BALL BOUNCE *(Second grade and up).* Each player has three chances to bounce a tennis ball into a trash basket sitting on a chair six feet away. No balls into the basket gets the player no prize. One or more balls into the basket gets one prize. All preschoolers get a consolation prize if no ball bounces into the waste basket.

OUTSIDE-INSIDE PARTY

Winter can be, well, boring. Cold day, cold snow, no sun. You get the picture. That's why people will love to pay to get into this winter party.

This fundraiser will not only raise money but people's spirits, too. Decorate a hall or large room so that it looks like a park in springtime. Bring in large potted plants and trees. These may be borrowed from local nurseries or businesses. Artificial turf can be rolled out for the grass. Garbage cans, picnic tables and "Please Don't Litter" signs will add to the atmosphere. Ants are optional. Plan summer games such as badminton, croquet and volleyball. Supplies can be borrowed or donated.

In your publicity for this wintertime picnic, encourage people to wear summer clothes. Inform them that hamburgers and hotdogs will be provided. Those attending are to provide the side dishes plus a donation or fixed admission fee. Food assignments can be made in the following way:

> A–E buns and condiments
> F–J chips and beans
> K–O salads: fruit, green, potato
> P–T desserts
> U–Z beverages

Promote this as a fun fundraiser to support your youth's upcoming mission or work-camp trip, and people will party to help others.

THE PAGEANT PURSE

Many churches sponsor Christmas and Easter pageants that are well-attended and enjoyed. Often, these events are done at no charge. Why not charge a small fee with the income going to a special youth ministry project? Tickets can be sold in advance and at the door. The cause to which the money is to be donated can be printed on the tickets, and during the program, young people can talk about what they will be doing, and ask for additional donations.

PIZZA PLACE ALL NIGHTER

If your community has a pizza parlor (with video games) large enough to hold a hundred or more young people, then this fundraiser may be for you. You can make arrangements with the establishment to close their doors at midnight on a Friday night (or on a weeknight during spring break). The night can be filled with pizza, movies, video games, board games and what-ever other activities your group would like.

From midnight until 2:00 A.M., free pizza is offered. The video games are open for free play all night. You can bring a big screen TV and VCR along with a couple of good video movies to show throughout the evening. Board games like monopoly can also be set up in a special tournament section of the store. A breakfast of donuts and juice can be served in the morning before the young people leave. The pizza business can figure out what it would cost them for the pizza, donuts, juice and an employee or two for the night plus profit and make you an offer. If you can double the amount and still get a large group of your young people to attend, you've got a great fundraiser and party wrapped into one. For example, if the store manager charges you eight dollars per person, you can charge sixteen dollars and with 100 young people in attendance, you would make $800. If you pay for a couple of adult workers to chaperon, you will still come out ahead and have fun as well. Parents are often willing to pay a little extra for an event if they know the proceeds are going to a worthy event.

If you are worried that not enough kids will show up, sell tickets in advance. You can estimate your attendance more accurately and guarantee the pizza store manager attendance of a certain number of young people as well.

A variation of this strategy that earns more money is to ask the kids to sell two to ten tickets to their grandparents, friends and neighbors. The tickets can sell for the same price as your all-nighter tickets even though those people will not be attending. You can finance an entire project through this one event.

SUNDAY SUNDAE FUN

Here's a family event that is sure to be a success. Everyone likes ice cream and this fundraiser offers that and more.

For this event you will need chocolate, vanilla and strawberry ice cream. Also, you will need a variety of toppings such as syrups, sprinkles, nuts, fruits, and whipped cream. Check with your local dairy or ice cream parlor about getting these items donated (in exchange for advertising) or purchase them at wholesale prices. You may be able to get sundae dishes, spoons and napkins donated from ice cream parlors as a promotional effort.

Advertise the event and sell tickets in advance so you will know how many you will be serving. You can sell tickets to people who plan on not attending. When a potential ticket holder balks at buying a ticket, explain your cause and ask for a ticket donation anyway.

Talented individuals from your group can provide the evening's enter-tainment. Taped background music also sets the mood. Have someone make a presentation on how the funds raised will be used and take an offering or ask for additional money. This can be done tactfully and in good taste. Don't be afraid to ask for money since you have a worthy cause that needs support. Asking for additional money offers the opportunity for people in attendance to further support your youth ministry.

Set all the ice cream toppings on a long covered table(s). Allow people assembling their sundaes to pass on both sides of the table so the line will move quickly.

Awards for the prettiest, messiest, most colorful, and strangest combination can be given. You may also wish to have a group sing or play ice cream related games like the ones below.

Cleanup is easy. Place large trash cans around the room. Each person can throw away his or her own disposables. Items that need to be washed can be placed in tubs to be washed and put away later.

SUNDAY SUNDAE FUN GAMES

As people arrive give them a colored name tag that not only tells others their name, but also determines what team they are on:

> Brown tags—the Chocolate Chips
> Red tags—the Straw Berries
> Green tags—the Pistachio Nuts
> Orange tags—the Orange Sherbets
> Yellow tags—the French Vanillas

After a few songs or mixers, break the group into teams and have fun with the following games:

YOU SCREAM, I SCREAM, WE ALL SCREAM FOR ICE CREAM. Each team creates its own team cheer based on its name. Winner should be judged on creativity, originality, humor and choreography.

CHERRY TOPPER RELAY. Each team lines up single file with everyone having one bare foot. Place a chair about twenty feet from the starting line with a pan of crushed ice and water with one maraschino cherry in it. Place an empty sundae dish beside it. Each contestant must run down, sit in the chair, fish out the cherry with his or her bare toes, place it in the sundae dish, race back, and tag the next person, who repeats the same activity. First team to successfully complete the relay wins.

BANANA PEEL. Get the captain of each team to take off his or her shoes and socks and sit facing the audience. Give them each a banana which he or she has to peel using only his or her feet and toes. First one to get it completely peeled is the winner.

NUT CRACKER RELAY. Each team member places a peanut between his or her knees and one at a time, waddles down to a sundae dish which is on the floor about ten feet from the start line. The object is for them to stand over the dish and try to make the peanut fall into it. If they miss, they simply pick up their peanut and get back in line to try again. If they drop their peanut before reaching the dish they have to go back to the starting line and begin again. The team that gets the most peanuts in the dish is the winner.

ICE CREAM CONE CARRY. Place a chair about thirty feet from each line. The first player on each team must walk down to the chair, go around it and come back while balancing an empty ice cream cone on top of his or her head. If it falls simply put it back on and keep going (unless it breaks, then get a new one). First team to have everyone successfully complete the task is the winner.

CHAPTER TWELVE

SERVICE PROJECTS

SOCIAL ACTION PROJECTS NEED TO BE FUNDED. Here you will find a few fundraising ideas related to service projects. Most of the ideas in this book can also be used to financially support social action and mission activities.

AGENCY FUNDRAISERS

Each of the following agencies has created informational programs that can help motivate your group to raise funds for world hunger and relief, self-help assistance, and child sponsorship.

COMPASSION INTERNATIONAL

P.O. Box 7000
Colorado Springs, CO 80933
(800) 336-7538

Provides "The Compassion Project," an educational program that will inform and challenge your youth group concerning the issues of hunger and poverty. Compassion has a sponsor-a-child program that will interest your group.

CROP
28606 Phillips Street
Elkhart, IN 46515
(219) 264-3102
A National Council of Churches organization that sponsors CROP walks to fight hunger.

FOOD FOR THE HUNGRY
7729 East Greenway Road
Scottsdale, AZ 85260
(602) 998-3100
Provide instructions and promotional literature for conducting a Starve-a-Thon.

HABITAT FOR HUMANITY
121 Habitat Street
Americus, GA 31709-3498
(912) 924-6541
Ask about their Habitat House Bank, a cardboard house that can be used for a countertop donation program to raise money for building homes and eliminating poverty.

WORLD VISION
P.O. Box 1131
Pasadena, CA 91131
(818) 357-7979
(800) 444-2522 for special programs like Planned Famine, Love Loaves, Countertops, as well as films/videos.
(800) 777-5777 for information on child sponsorship, relief and development in Third World countries, emergency aid, and assistance in church outreach.

BRINGING IN THE SHEAVES
Here's a simple, low-cost way to line up food and provisions for a work camp or service project. This way the money you raised for your camp or project can be used for other things. Just make up your menu, prepare a shopping list, and post the items needed on a sign-up sheet in your church. Include instructions about when and where to leave donated items. This is a practical approach to stretching a tight service project budget.

2 gallons potato salad _____

2 dozen hamburger buns _____

1 small jar mustard _____

1 large onion _____

2 heads lettuce _____

2 packages chips _____

2 packages chips _____

2 gallons milk _____

2 gallons milk _____

2 loaves wheat bread _____

2 loaves white bread _____

2 loaves French bread _____

4 dozen eggs _____

10 lbs. oranges _____

5 lbs. bananas _____

2 boxes cold cereal _____

2 packages lunch meats _____

2 packages lunch meats _____

1 12-oz. pkg. cheese slices _____

1 12-oz. pkg. cheese slices _____

1 quart jam _____

2 dozen sweet rolls _____

2 large cans vegetable soup _____

hot cocoa mix _____

GLEANING FOR GOLD

God commanded the Israelite farmers to allow orphans, widows, the poor, and strangers to go through the fields after the harvest to glean usable food left by the harvesters (Lev. 19:9–10; Deut. 24:19). This same practice can be used by your group to help orphans, widows, the poor and the homeless.

Obtain permission from farmers, orchard growers, gardeners or anyone else in agriculture to glean their fields. Also, ask people you know who have gardens to donate ten percent of their produce to your cause. Have your kids collect the usable food and sell it to members of your church or organization. A portion of the collected food can be given to your local food bank. The money you raise can go to support your other service projects.

Your county extension agent may be able to provide your group with advice and help in identifying farms that would be open to gleaning.

HOLIDAY GIFT CERTIFICATES

If your group has an upcoming service project over the holidays, sell "Holiday Gift Certificates" to people who wish to sponsor a holiday service project. Purchasers of the certificates are buying an hour of a youth's service, plus supplies, for a specified amount of money. Be sure you give a report to the donors after the project is completed.

INVEST-IN-A-SERVANT

Here's a fun and creative service project that also raises money for your group's other service projects. Have the young people solicit pledges for a two hour period of service. Each young person creates his or her own service project that can be done within the two hour time period (this can also be done in groups of two to five young people). These projects can include helping out at a food bank, doing yard work for the elderly people, sorting clothes at a rescue mission, and the like. The personal service project can be presented to people in the community to solicit the pledges.

Synchronize the two hour service projects on a day and time when all the young people can get together afterward to discuss what they learned from the experience.

MEAL-A-THON

This Pledge-a-Thon combines a fundraiser with a service project. You can use it when your group is raising money to combat world hunger, homelessness, or poverty. Contact your local Salvation Army, soup kitchen, church, or social service agency that feeds the homeless in your area. Ask if your group can donate their time to make sack lunches, prepare food or help in whatever that agency does to feed the homeless. Your group can prepare the meals and serve them to the homeless. (This is important. Don't rob your young people of this privilege to have direct contact with those in need.) The money is made in the pledges that your group takes from people for every sack lunch packed and delivered, or plate of food prepared, or whatever your group does.

PROJECT DOOR KNOB

Distribute flyers around the community announcing that on a certian date your youth group will be passing by in the church bus or van looking for work to do. If anyone wishes help, they simply tie a handkerchief onto the doorknob of their front door. You can charge a flat fee for this service or ask for donations. With several young people working together, the work gets done quickly. At the end of your work session, you can throw a party. You'll be amazed at how many people will take advantage of this offer.

SEASONAL SERVANTS

The following seasonal jobs can be done as a group. Simply get a group together, go door-to-door, and ask people if they want the seasonal job done. A group member acts as a spokesperson, explaining the group's cause and requesting a donation for the service. More money can be made when the group goes to homes or businesses where a group member(s) knows the occupants or owners. After the work is done, your group can throw a party of their own planning to celebrate a good day's work done.

#1 RAKE AND RUN. Each group member brings his or her own rake. Several young people working together can rake and bag a yard full of leaves in a matter of minutes.

#2 SNOW AND BLOW. Instead of rakes your group members bring snow shovels and clear people's sidewalks.

#3 SPLASH AND SPLIT. Your group brings rags and window cleaner to clean the windows of homes and businesses. Since people hate washing their windows, this can be a real money-maker. And windows can be washed quickly with a number of young people working as a team.

#4 MOW AND BLOW. Young people mow lawns, pull weeds, and do other chores that go with lawn mowing.

SOCK GIVE-AWAY

This year, don't bless the socks off the needy in your community. Bless the needy with socks! Decorate shoe boxes with a sock motif and place them throughout the church. By means of signs and flyers, ask those who attend church or Sunday school to donate money so that the youth group can purchase socks to be given to needy children through an approved community agency. After three weeks, the group goes shopping for socks with the money collected.

The following week, decorate your meeting room with socks—old socks, new socks, Christmas socks, huge socks, teeny socks—and display in some way the socks the group purchased to give away. If dancing is appropriate, you can celebrate the collection effort with a sock hop (everyone must wear socks they decorated at home). Offer crazy prizes for the prettiest, ugliest, scariest, and funniest socks. Then turn up some oldies and dance the limbo, the twist, and the pony. The day after the sock hop, give the new socks to the agency.

SOUP KITCHEN

If your church wants to help feed the hungry, but you're in an area where there aren't enough needy people to warrant a soup kitchen, try this idea. Set up a "market table" in the fellowship hall or a Sunday school room where church members bring produce from their own gardens for other members to buy. Items can be purchased for a freewill donation rather than a set price.

The money raised from this project can then be sent to help support a soup kitchen in another area. Though the market table involves only a minimum of preparation and organization, it can generate a useful sum for ministry to the hungry.

SUPPLY SCAVENGER HUNT

If your group is planning a mission trip that requires donated supplies—tools, building materials, clothing, and the like—consider having a Supply Scavenger Hunt a few weeks before the trip. Send your young people into the community with a list similar to the one on this page and you will be amazed at how many good, usable items your kids will bring back. It's a worthwhile activity—and fun, too!

Dear Friend:

We need the following supplies for our First Church work camp in _____. Anything you can donate will be greatly appreciated.

Thank you!

- hammer
- rake
- work gloves (any condition)
- rubber concrete gloves
- pick (of any sort)
- plastic safety goggles
- brownies or chocolate-chip cookies
- hoe (any condition)
- one box of framing nails
- concrete trowel (any style)
- wheelbarrow
- shovel
- drop cloths
- paint brushes

TEEN TITHING

We need to become more intentional in creatively teaching young people to tithe. Young people earn more money than many adults realize (billions of business dollars are spent targeting the youth market). Why wait until they are adults to promote tithing?

The mistake the church often makes in promoting tithing among the young is asking them to give, but not involving them in where and how the money is spent. Here are only a few ideas for creatively involving your young people.

- Take the church's budget, ask the youth group to review it and discuss their findings with the church treasurer and other board members.
- Ask the youth group to design their own church budget.

■ Schedule a panel of regular tithers to come and hold a question-and-answer session with your young people about giving.

■ Ask the ushers to bring the offering into your Sunday school classroom, set it on a table and, while the young people are looking at the money, talk about tithing and stewardship. (To protect anonymity, don't let the kids see the checks.)

■ Have youth group members interview church staff (and volunteers) on how they put together a budget.

■ Ask the group to create a budget for the next retreat or camp.

■ Challenge your group to pick an ongoing project that they can financially support with their own money—not fundraised money but from their personal allowances and earnings.

■ Compute with the youth group how much money the average youth group member may make in a lifetime, and how much they will, on average, give to God.

■ Talk with the youth group about the spiritual discipline of thrift.

WINTERIZE YOUR ELDERLY

Raking leaves is only the beginning of what needs to be done for the shut-ins and the elderly of your church, especially if you live in cold-weather country. Before cold weather sets in, your group's teens can put up storm windows, change furnace filters, haul in patio furniture, take down porch awnings—difficult or impossible chores for the elderly, but just a few hours of work for energetic young people.

And don't forget them the following spring when the houses must be returned to warm-weather condition and the lawns mowed.

Those elderly who can afford the service will probably be happy to pay; for those who can't, your group members can find sponsors to support the work. Your group raises money for your cause and helps those who are unable to help themselves maintain their homes.

CHAPTER THIRTEEN

IDEAS FOR PROMOTION AND PUBLICITY

THE BEST-LAID PLANS NEED PEOPLE TO FUND THEM. And the funds won't come in unless the people do. You may have a worthy cause, but unless you effectively promote your fundraiser, it will quickly turn into a fund-loser. Hit-and-miss promotional efforts lead to unsupported events and little money raised for your cause. On the other hand, a well-planned and executed event can raise thousands of dollars. When publicity becomes an integral part of your planning, you are more likely to have a successful money-maker. And publicity for your fundraiser has the added benefit of promoting your organization or group and your cause.

We recommend that you elect one of your youth to be a fundraising publicity leader. One or two volunteers who can motivate your group members and oversee your promotional efforts will prove to be a tremendous benefit to your fundraising efforts.

BE A GUEST

Get invited to be a guest on a local radio (or TV) talk show. If you have a newsworthy story, you may find the free publicity you receive a big boost to your upcoming fundraiser. Since these shows often schedule guests weeks and even months in advance, contact them early.

BIG MOUTHS

Examine most fundraisers and you will find the single most effective publicity is word of mouth. You can help your group members become more effective and intentional at being "big mouths" for your fundraisers by providing them with information in the form of flyers and posters as well as practiced presentations.

You can also, as a group, set a goal for each of the young people and adults in your group to tell ten people (or whatever number you choose) about your project within a specified time. You can practice, through role-plays, a presentation that includes the details of your fundraiser such as day, time, place and for what purpose the money is being raised.

BUSINESS BILLS

Creating small handbills that can be placed in the lobbies or high traffic areas of local businesses can effectively spread the word about your event. You can target large numbers of potential supporters by placing a flyer at your local supermarket, doctors' offices, bookstores, etc. Church youth groups can reach potential supporters by placing posters and flyers at their local Christian bookstores. Many businesses are willing to advertise a fundraiser that supports a worthy cause.

BUTTON BOOSTERS

Buttons that can be worn by group members to church, school and work have proven to be inexpensive and valuable marketing tools. A little creativity and a button-making machine is all you need for your group to wear advertising wherever they go.

You can order a machine through Badge A Minit, 348 N. 30th Rd., Box 800, LaSalle, IL 61301, or call (800) 223-4103.

CELEBRITY ATTENTION

Enlist the support of big-time movie and rock music personalities. How? You can usually obtain the life-size posters that are used by theater, movie-rental and music stores to advertise new movies and records. If you talk to the managers of these businesses, they will give these to your group, once their own advertising campaigns are completed.

You can then take these life-size posters and create your own promotional campaign by having the stars say something about your fundraiser. For example, you could have a life-sized Amy Grant saying "Can we count on you to support . . . ?" You get the picture.

CHEAP CLASSIFIEDS

Most communities have a *Penny Saver*-type classified newspaper (ours is called *The Dandy Dime*) in which your group can place inexpensive (and sometimes free) ads. These are effective in promoting events like auctions and special events.

COUNT THE WAYS

A good publicity campaign that gets results includes a number of different types of promotion. People need multiple exposures to your upcoming event in today's world of media bombardment. You need to tell people what you are doing, remind them that you are doing it, jog their memory a time or two, and then tell them again so they will not forget. A good rule of thumb is the seven time rule: Tell people in seven different ways to guarantee adequate promotion. Here is a partial list of promotional strategies:

- newsletters (yours and others')
- church bulletins
- flyers
- posters
- newspaper stories
- verbal announcements
- letters
- postcards
- signs
- sandwich boards
- marquees
- personal invitations
- calendars (yours and others')
- mailings
- telephone trees

CRAZY ANNOUNCEMENTS

Inject a little craziness into those monotonous support-our-fundraiser announcements. Write a song, produce a funny skit, dress in an outlandish outfit, play charades, create a goofy game show—anything out of the ordinary that people will remember. For example, if you are selling stock (see Bullish On The Youth Group, page 35), you could dress as a stockbroker with ticker tape wrapped around your neck, briefcase and portfolios in hand.

CREATIVE GRAPHICS

Computer technology, low-cost clip art, and other creative aids have made schlock flyers and newsletters a thing of the past. Take advantage of these tools. Never let anything go out of your office that looks unprofessional. The efforts you make on behalf of young people need to be first class. They deserve nothing less.

DROP CLOTH DISPLAY

A painter's canvass drop cloth provides an excellent portable wall on which to create an inexpensive promotional billboard that can be used again and again. Ask at your local paint store for the best type of paint to use on the type of drop cloth you purchase—then create away. You can bring out your billboard whenever and wherever it is needed, then neatly store it away to be used at another time.

ENTRY FORMS

Create an entry form that generates interest and serves as a publicity form as well. Entry forms provide a method for your group members to approach potential donors. Creatively done, these offer you the chance to sign up more people for your event. They can also be placed at businesses and given to other groups to be offered to a wider audience than your own church or organization.

FACTOIDS

An attractive (but inexpensively done) fact sheet or brochure explaining who your group is, what it does, and where donation dollars are going, gives group members a fundraising tool. When young people present the giving opportunity to donors, they can use the fact sheet to support their appeal. Fact sheets and brochures also force your group to put in writing why you are raising money. And that in itself is an exercise that can help your group raise more money because you have defined the whats, whys, and hows.

FREEBIE POSTER BOARD

Your group can save money on publicity by asking local merchants (music stores, video rental stores, department stores, fast-food restaurants, grocery stores) to save the posters in their windows for you. You can use the reverse sides of these poster boards to create your own poster. You have done your recycling duty and saved yourself money on materials as well.

HOMEMADE VIDEO

Your group can create their own personalized video using a home video camera and a little creativity. Add music and graphics if you can. Your group members can show the video as part of a presentation to groups who are potential donors.

LONG DISTANCE LETTER

This is a great publicity idea for church and para-church groups raising money for a mission trip or support for a missionary. Ask different missionaries in foreign countries that your group supports or are in contact with to write a letter asking people to support your fundraiser. This letter can be read during a church service, Sunday school classes, or a special event. People are always impressed when they hear from another country.

MAKING NEWS

Your group can get free publicity from your local media through local radio, TV, and print outlets. If your fundraising event and the project it supports are newsworthy, write a press release and attract the attention of the media. You can send a press release to school newspapers, weekly community papers, Christian radio stations, weekly shoppers, organizational newsletters, local magazines, and local cable TV stations as well as your city newspapers, television stations and pop radio stations. You can get the best results through personal meetings with editors and program managers. You often can get a commitment for print stories or air time when you have the opportunity for face-to-face contact. And don't forget to bring pictures of last year's event!

FOR IMMEDIATE RELEASE

Youth In Action

Santa Ana Christian High School Youth In Action
4256 West La Canada Drive
Tucson, Arizona 85705

Contact: Jonathan Wells, Chapter President
555-1649

FOR IMMEDIATE RELEASE

Santa Ana Christian High School, September 10, 19—
Youth In Action, with the city food bank, is sponsoring a Starve-a-Thon all night Friday, October 7, 19—. All the money raised will be used to fight hunger in Tucson. Last year, Youth In Action raised over $3,000. The students participating in the Starve-a-Thon are gathering sponsors from around the Tucson community. They will spend the night at Santa Ana Christian High to learn more about and plan strategies to feed the hungry of Tucson in the name of Jesus Christ.

Anyone interested in sponsoring a student can call the school at 555-1649. All money will be donated to the food bank where the students are working to make a difference in Tucson. Youth In Action is a club created by the students of Santa Ana Christian High School to help the needy in the Tucson community.

ON THE SPOT PR

Give your group and participants a break from those boring old name tags. At your next event where you need name tags, try one of the following:

- Use the hats given out at some fast-food restaurants. They can be turned inside out and written on.
- Create name tag buttons with decorations (see Button Boosters on page 135).
- Paint a message like "Ask me, I like to help" on the back of old work shirts.
- Face paint the names of your helpers.

PSA

Public Service Announcements are another means of gaining media exposure for your fundraising event. Your group can write a PSA about your good cause that lasts ten to sixty seconds. Then contact your TV and radio stations and submit your announcement to be added to their regular roster of Public Service Announcements.

REMEMBER LAST YEAR

If you repeat projects year after year like a camp or mission trip, take advantage of this built-in promotional opportunity. You can use pictures and videos from last year's event as a publicity tool for this year's event. Put together a commercial that illustrates what your group has done in the past and will do again this year. A great visual tool produced from last year's event can promote giving for this year's.

TICKET SALES

Guarantee your group paying donors, and promote your event at the same time by selling tickets in advance. Tickets make it easier for your group members to approach potential givers. You can better gauge how many people will be attending your event and may even get people who don't plan to attend to purchase tickets.

Don't forget to print the purpose of your fundraiser on the ticket. People are more willing to give when the cause is well defined.

CHAPTER FOURTEEN

PUBLISHING PROJECTS

HOT-OFF-THE-PRESS DOLLARS CAN BE MADE with the following publishing projects. If your group has a ready market, a little creativity and a need for money, consider one or more of the following publication ideas.

BOOK BLAST

Have the youth group write a book. Tap the creative potential of the group and have the kids write stories, poetry, articles, and essays, or submit cartoons, drawings, and anything else that can be reproduced. Have it all edited by a committee, pasted up and printed by the "offset" process. (Photos can be included this way.) You may have members of your group or church that have experience in desk-top publishing who will help. A local printer or bindery can bind your book. Select a catchy title and design a nice cover which can be printed or silk-screened on cover stock. The books can then be advertised and sold in the church and community.

CHURCH BIRTHDAY/ANNIVERSARY CALENDAR

Here's an idea that has successfully raised thousands of dollars over the years. What you do is sell people in your church anniversary and birthday dates on a calendar.

There are now computer programs that create twelve-month calendars. Find the program as well as a person who can use it. Then place the names of all the people whom you have sold space to on the appropriate dates for the upcoming year. These calendar months can then be photocopied and stapled together, or you can sell ads in the calendar to local businesses to cover the cost of printing and go first class.

Begin selling dates on the calendar in September. People pay one dollar per date (birthday, anniversary or both) to have their name printed in the calendar. Those same people are now potential customers to buy the calendars in November and December for three to five dollars. Promote this as a fundraiser with proceeds going to a specific cause, and people will be happy to give twice. Remember to add the dates of important church events and holidays. Place the birth dates and anniversaries of church shut-ins at no charge.

Create a simple entry form. A booth set up in the lobby or narthex of your church is a good place to solicit business. Schools can solicit names through their student bodies. Youth organizations can sell to members' families.

People will look forward to buying a date and purchasing the calendar every year. An easy money-maker with high repeat success.

Valley Church Birthday & Anniversary Calendar Entry Form

BIRTHDAY ($1.00 donation requested)

Full Name _____
FIRST   MIDDLE (OPTIONAL)   LAST

Birth Date _____
MONTH AND DAY ONLY (NO YEARS)

- -

ANNIVERSARY ($1.00 donation requested)

Couple's Name _____

Anniversary _____
MONTH   DAY   YEAR MARRIED

CO-OP COOKBOOK

Take the "Recipe Fundraiser" (below) on the road by collaborating with a number of other youth groups in putting together a cookbook. Five church youth groups can each collect recipes from their respective churches. Each group can take responsibility for a section of the cookbook. For example, First Church takes appetizers, Central Avenue Church covers beverages, Victory Church collects salad recipes, Eastside Church seeks main dishes, and St. John's handles desserts.

Take the names of contributors and print their names and church with their recipe. Be sure to remember to inform people who submit recipes as to their purpose and get permission to publish them.

MISSION TRIP PACKETS

You can put together packets that describe your upcoming mission trip or work camp that can be sold to prospective investors in your mission program. Packets can include a youth group brochure, the purpose of the trip, goals of the trip, a trip itinerary, a list of prayer needs and the like. Use the packets as a tool to sell people on funding the trip.

RECIPE FUNDRAISER

Have your youth group collect recipes from anyone in or out of the group or church, then organize them into sections with the contributor's name at the bottom of each recipe. The recipes are printed and put in a semi-hard or hardcover notebook. Depending on the number of recipes, you can sell each book for five to fifteen dollars. People are always looking for recipes and these will sell fast. You can use the recipe form on page 146 to gather recipes from your cook contributors.

Recipe Form

Your Name _____

Address _____

Phone Number _____

Title of Recipe _____

Category _____

(soup, main dish, dessert, etc.)

INGREDIENTS

_____

_____

_____

_____

_____

PREPARATION

_____

_____

_____

_____

_____

_____

_____

YIELD _____

YELLOW PAGE DIRECTORIES

Your group can raise money by publishing its own "yellow pages" to sell to church members. Individual business listings in the directory can sell for five to fifty dollars (or more) to local merchants and professionals, especially those in the church. In addition, the youth can include their own listings for yard work, babysitting, and other jobs.

Typing and compiling into alphabetical categories can be done by the youth themselves with a little adult help. Directories can be given to church members with a donation request, thus providing them with a useful service as well as raising funds for your program. A youth group used this idea and raised over one thousand dollars.

CHAPTER FIFTEEN

IDEAS FOR BETTER MANAGEMENT

THE FOLLOWING IDEAS ARE DESIGNED TO STRENGTHEN your fundraising management skills. You can begin your own list of ideas by documenting what you learn after each fundraiser in which you are involved. We also recommend that you find mentors with experience in fundraising who are willing to share their expertise with you.

ATTITUDE OF GRATITUDE

Here are some follow-up ideas to show appreciation to your donors. Choose the ones you feel would be most appropriate for your youth group, or create your own after reviewing the examples we have provided. Whatever you choose needs to demonstrate your group's gratitude for the gift as well as to bring the donor closer to your group and its cause.

#1 PERSONALIZED THANK-YOU CARD. Many givers experience a post-giving anxiety. It is like the jitters one gets after ordering something through the mail. Donors worry about the wisdom of giving what they did, no matter how small the gift. A personalized thank-you letter can go a long way to relieve this anxiety. Have the young people write the letters and include a little bit about your youth organization and how the money is to be spent. This helps affirm the wisdom of the gift in the mind of the donor. They can see concrete evidence of their resources being put to work.

#2 DONOR MAILING LIST. Keep donors apprised of what is going on by placing them on your mailing list. You can send them a postcard or letter informing them that they are being placed on your list as a result of their gift. Once a year, all donors can be surveyed to see if they wish to remain on your list. This list of donors can also be used for future fundraising appeals.

#3 GRATITUDE PHONE CALL. Recognize your givers through a phone call. Your kids can participate in this appreciation call. Before the phone calls of gratitude for the donation are made, train your young people (role-plays are a great training device) on phone etiquette and what must be communicated. Your givers can hear firsthand how their money will be spent and will appreciate talking with a young person, something most adults don't get a chance to do.

#4 PRAYER LIST. Create a prayer list that all donors receive with information about your projects and people for whom they are praying.

#5 GRATITUDE RECEIPT. Provide a receipt for the giver. People are accustomed to receiving receipts for things of value they have purchased. What a great way to demonstrate to donors that they have invested in something valu-

able. You can create your own or use the one we have provided on page
152. The sample Gratitude Receipt can be creatively dressed up by adding
a heart or picture of the youth group in the background.

DOLLAR-SAVING DONATIONS

You may not need to raise as much money as you think. Before you crank
up your fundraiser, find out if you can obtain what you need through donations. Here are some examples of what churches and other youth-serving
organizations have done to seek out donated services and materials needed to carry out their missions.

■ If you pay the expenses of adult youth workers (cost of youth group out-
ing, camp), check with them to see if they would be willing to pay their own
way. Many adult youth workers, if they can afford it, are more than willing
to help in this way.

■ Take advantage of such ideas as the Supply Scavenger Hunt (page 130) or
Bringing In The Sheaves (page 124) to acquire the supplies your group
needs.

■ Get rental vehicles donated for big trips your group plans to take. This is
easier than you think, especially if the purpose of your trip is clearly spelled
out and worthy of community support.

■ Get a tank of gas donated for those same trips.

■ Look for ways your group can obtain donated items to help others. One
group began approaching stores and bakeries that normally threw away
unsold food. The donated food was used to feed homeless people. For
example, they went to a cookie company that was glad to donate their
unsold cookies. They had not done so in the past because no one had
asked, and they had never thought anyone could use day-old cookies.

■ Take advantage of the easy-to-do Eco-Cash (page 93ff.) ideas. Collecting
cans or paper as a fundraising project, once it has been organized,
becomes easy cash that helps redeem God's creation.

Gratitude Receipt

Name _____

Address _____

City/State/Zip _____

Date Received _____

Contribution for

_____

Donation Amount: $_____

Thank you for your gift!

All contributions are tax deductible in the U.S.A.

KEEP THIS FOR YOUR RECORDS

Please feel free to photocopy and use this page.

Donated items make good sense, especially in a throwaway society that too quickly wastes the resources God has so abundantly blessed us with. A little imagination and group brainstorming will give you an abundance of ideas that can save you dollars.

EFFECTIVENESS FORMULA

Here's a simple step-by-step formula for calculating if you have a "worth doing" fundraiser.

1. Estimate the *total* amount of volunteer and paid staff hours necessary to raise the money.

    Staff Hours = _____

2. Calculate the dollar amount your group will *most likely* raise.

    Potential Dollars = _____

3. Divide the staff hours into the amount of money you expect to raise. This is the per-hour fundraising rate.

    Potential Dollars ÷ Staff Hours = _____

4. The higher the hourly wage, the better you are doing. No one wants his or her fundraiser to earn minimum wage, yet many fundraisers do this and worse. Take a look at the hourly wage and decide if you feel the fundraiser is worth the time and effort for your volunteer and paid staff.

An example can be seen in the selling of Christmas trees. We know of two groups who have sold Christmas trees during the holiday season. One is a YMCA and the other is a church youth group. Let's find out if their fundraisers were worth doing.

YMCA CHRISTMAS TREE SALE. The lot is open every day for three weeks from 10 A.M. to 10 P.M. There are two volunteers at the lot during the week and five on the weekends. There is also the set-up and tear down time that includes fencing, lighting, loading and unloading of trees plus advertising time and soliciting businesses for donations.

1. Staff Hours = 400

2. Dollars Netted = $8,000

3. $\dfrac{\$8,000 \text{ Netted}}{400 \text{ Staff Hours}}$ = $20.00 per hour

4. $\dfrac{\text{Dollars Netted}}{\text{Staff Hours}}$ = Yes, it's worth it! Not only was money raised for their after-school program, but they used the event as an excellent opportunity to promote their organization.

CHURCH CHRISTMAS TREE SALE. The church Christmas tree lot required somewhat less hours than the YMCA lot but still involved a considerable amount of time and work.

1. Staff Hours = 275

2. Dollars Netted = $1,700

3. $\dfrac{\$1,700 \text{ Netted}}{275 \text{ Staff Hours}}$ = $6.18 per hour

4. $\dfrac{\text{Dollars Netted}}{\text{Staff Hours}}$ = Is this good stewardship of staff and volunteer time? What other fundraising idea could be employed to net the same amount of money, but with less work?

FUNDRAISING ANNUAL PLAN

Planning your fundraising activities on a yearly basis is always a good idea. You can use the planning sheet found on page 156 to help you organize your annual calendar. When you use a tool such as this, you capture the bigger picture of what is happening with your fundraising efforts. We recommend you keep these year after year as an evaluation tool.

PENNY PINCHERS

Take some time with your group to go over your church's or organization's budget to look for ways that money can be saved. Your group, in addition to raising money, can become more conscious and intentional in saving money. And that is just as good as going out and raising extra money. You might discover ways to lower the number of photocopies made, conserve electricity, reduce phone bills, save on supplies, reduce heating and cooling costs, lower the cost of transportation, reduce the cost of facility maintenance, lower entertainment costs—the list is nearly endless.

Annual Fundraising "Big Picture" Plan

YEAR _____ DATE _____ DOLLAR GOAL $ _____

PROJECT	PROJECT LEADER(S)	LAST YEAR'S GOAL/ACTUAL		THIS YEAR'S GOAL	COLLECTED TO DATE	COMMENTS
1.	1.	1. $_____	1. $_____	1. $_____	1. $_____	1.
2.	2.	2. $_____	2. $_____	2. $_____	2. $_____	2.
3.	3.	3. $_____	3. $_____	3. $_____	3. $_____	3.
4.	4.	4. $_____	4. $_____	4. $_____	4. $_____	4.
5.	5.	5. $_____	5. $_____	5. $_____	5. $_____	5.
6.	6.	6. $_____	6. $_____	6. $_____	6. $_____	6.
7.	7.	7. $_____	7. $_____	7. $_____	7. $_____	7.
8.	8.	8. $_____	8. $_____	8. $_____	8. $_____	8.
9.	9.	9. $_____	9. $_____	9. $_____	9. $_____	9.
10.	10.	10. $_____	10. $_____	10. $_____	10. $_____	10.

Please feel free to photocopy and use this page.

GREAT FUNDRAISING IDEAS

INDEX